AN AMERICAN KNIGHT

The Life of Colonel John W. Ripley, USMC

AmericanKnight.org

by

Norman J. Fulkerson

THE AMERICAN SOCIETY FOR THE DEFENSE
OF TRADITION, FAMILY AND PROPERTY—TFP
SPRING GROVE, PENN. 17362

Cover: Colonel John W. Ripley, USMC./ Photo by Anthony
Edgeworth/EdgeworthEditions.

Copyright© 2011 The American Society for the Defense of Tradition,
Family and Property®—TFP®
1358 Jefferson Road, Spring Grove, PA 17362 • (866) 661-0272
www.TFP.org

Design: Jennifer Bohdal
2nd edition, third printing.

The American Society for the Defense of Tradition, Family and Property®
and TFP® are registered names of The Foundation for a Christian
Civilization, Inc., a 501(c)(3) tax-exempt organization.

ISBN-13: 978-1-877905-41-4
ISBN-10: 1-877905-41-0
Library of Congress Control Number: 2009909762

Printed in the United States of America

*To the Mother of God and Her champion,
Saint Michael, the prototype warrior who
vanquished the first Revolutionary and,
by so doing, became the model for all
warriors throughout history.*

AN AMERICAN KNIGHT

The Life of Colonel John W. Ripley, USMC

PRAISE FOR
AN AMERICAN KNIGHT

"To those privileged to know him well, John Ripley unquestionably manifested many of the personal and professional characteristics and qualities associated with the noblest of those who are called to the profession of arms. He was, indeed, a modern day knight, and a Marine leader well above "standard issue." Marines idolize the icons of our Corps: Lejeune, Puller, Daly, and a few others. History should, and I have no doubt will, include John Ripley on that short list. He stands tall among the best of the best who bear the title Marine.

"Norman Fulkerson has produced a fine book which provides well-deserved tribute to a great man."
— **General Carl E. Mundy, USMC (Ret.),**
30ᵗʰ Commandant of the Marine Corps

"I knew Colonel John W. Ripley like a brother for 42 plus years, but the facts are that I learned still more about my Marine buddy from Norman Fulkerson's book *An American Knight*. Norman goes into family and early life details that started this Marine on his most successful Marine career as well as John's perception of the obligation and performance of his duties in uniform. This is a "must read" for all desiring to be a leader, especially those desiring to lead Marines."
— **Colonel Wesley Lee Fox, USMC (Ret.),**
Medal of Honor Recipient,
Author of *Marine Rifleman: Forty-three*
Years in the Corps* and *Courage and Fear

"*An American Knight* by Norman Fulkerson is an outstanding tribute to one of the finest men to ever wear a uniform of the United States of America."
— **Commander Paul Galanti, USN (Ret.),**
POW for seven years

"In his new book *An American Knight*, Norman Fulkerson has vividly captured the extraordinary active journey in life of Colonel. John Ripley. In this first ever biography, of a truly legendary Marine, the reader will see a man of many images; a gentle person who was comfortable with people of all stations of life, a caring father, a faithful husband, and a Marine capable of doing the seemingly impossible when I ordered him to destroy the Dong Ha Bridge.

"Because of his compelling and uncommon level of service to this great nation, Colonel John Ripley truly deserves to be held up as a role model for all to follow. Norman Fulkerson's book will help ensure this."
— Colonel Gerald Turley, USMC (Ret.),
Author of *The Easter Offensive*

"I attended the Officers Basic School and the Naval War College with John Ripley and got to know and admire him as a truly professional combat warrior. His heroics and leadership are legendary.

"After reading *An American Knight*, I realize the strong foundation upon which he built his life from childhood, to marriage, to a dedicated life as a United States Marine. John Ripley, the total man, dedicated his every breath to his God, his family, his country and his beloved Marine Corps. I was honored to call him my friend."
— Colonel H. C. "Barney" Barnum Jr. USMC (Ret.)
Medal of Honor Recipient

"While the world knew my brother John as a Navy Cross recipient, I will always remember him simply as my darling little boy. Being the oldest member of our family I had the joy of caring for him as if he were my own child. It was for this reason that I was overjoyed when Norman Fulkerson contacted me, after John's death, with the idea of writing a book about his life.

"The final product, titled *An American Knight*, gave me the chance to see a side of John I frankly never knew. Although I was well aware of his heroism at Dong Ha, I did not know he was such a legend in the Marine Corps, because he did not tell me those things. John was very humble.

"While I thoroughly enjoyed *An American Knight* and found it to be an extremely accurate account of my brother's life, it was, at the same time, a painful read since it brought back so many happy memories of someone I sorely miss. I have had, since John's death, this feeling that he would never die. That is to say that his memory would live forever. Now I know it certainly will because of Mr. Fulkerson's book."

"On behalf of my family, of which I am the last living member, I say thank you!"
— Mary Susan Goodykoontz

CONTENTS

FOREWORD

It is safe to say that since the dawn of history no warrior has captured man's imagination as much as the medieval knight. Images of chargers frothing at the mouth as they propel their steel-clad riders into the fray will likely fascinate mankind until the end of time.

However, these knights were known for more than their wartime deeds alone. They also personified the Christian virtues to a high degree. They are the stuff of which legends are made!

Thus, anyone who tries to compare any modern man with these mythical warriors has his work cut out for him. However, this is the task which Norman Fulkerson has striven to accomplish in the present book. In it, he recounts the crib-to-grave story of Colonel John W. Ripley, making *An American Knight: The Life of Colonel John W. Ripley, USMC* an engaging read that will be hard to put down, regardless of the reader's background.

Having known Colonel Ripley personally, I can affirm that if there are still men who merit the title "knight," he is one of them.

We were fellow Marines and shared that friendship which unites all warriors who have struggled together and shed their blood on the same fields. In fact, the Colonel and I fought literally on the same battlefield, as, on April 30, 1968, I was ordered to defend the Dong Ha Bridge in the Quang Tri Province of Vietnam. Ironically, Colonel Ripley would earn a Navy Cross four years later by destroying that same bridge. Because of that fact, I would often tease him, complaining that he had: "destroyed my bridge!" However, my story had little to do with Dong Ha.

Rather, on May 2, 1968, I led 180 Marines of E Company in an assault on the hamlet of Dai Do to relieve G Company that was stranded there. They had been separated from the rest of their battalion and were facing a situation that was getting desperate in a hurry. To accomplish our mission, we had to advance across a 500-meter-long rice paddy, under heavy enemy fire without any cover. On the way, we cleared more than one hundred A-frame bunkers which could only be taken by getting close enough to blow them up from the inside—a difficult task, considering each one contained a fresh North Vietnamese soldier hell-bent on keeping his bunker intact.

After securing Dai Do, my force of 180 had shrunk to thirty-seven Marines. All the others had been killed or wounded. A few hours later, I heard over the radio that H Company, which was besieging a town within a couple hundred yards of my position, was in trouble. I then ordered my men to reenter the fray in support of H Company. In spite of everything they had been through, every one of those thirty-seven Marines unhesitatingly responded: "Yes sir!"

We ran the couple hundred yards to H Company's position and got back into the fight. Shortly after, I received a .50 caliber bullet in my leg that incapacitated me. I proceeded to offer cover fire for my men to get them to safety, telling them to move on and leave me where I lay. Two courageous Marines disobeyed my orders, approached me and said: "Skipper, you're coming with us."

They evacuated me and, after two months in the hospital, I was back on my feet. I received the Medal of Honor for my actions that day from President Richard Nixon, on May 14, 1970.

With this background, it is understandable that I would read avidly *An American Knight*. However, I was surprised to find in it, a book that is attractive to any reader because it highlights a variety of Colonel Ripley's qualities both in combat and out.

This is indispensable if one sets out to compare him to our medieval predecessors, because being a knight meant a lot more than prowess on the battlefield. It meant upright and gentlemanly conduct, the practice of the Faith, care for the weak and defenseless, and a whole slew of other characteristics that the Colonel possessed.

Particularly noteworthy is the moral courage he showed by taking controversial stances against allowing women in combat and homosexuals in the military. In doing so, he confronted intense pressure to capitulate, but stood true to his convictions.

Thus, he lived up to his own idea of bravery which he believed was more praiseworthy when practiced in defense of one's principles in face of hostility than against the enemy on a battlefield. "I have seen courage in many forms," he said, "but that which I admire far more than physical courage is moral courage, which I define as the will to stick up for your moral and ethical principles when someone turns up the heat."

This moral integrity demonstrates a similarity between Colonel Ripley and the medieval knight, but so does his style of leadership in battle. Like his armored forbearers, the Colonel led his troops from the front lines. This corresponds with my idea of leadership and the way I always led my men. Simply put, an effective combat commander must be close enough to the fighting to "smell the gunpowder." If he cannot do that, he is simply too far away.

Colonel Ripley practiced this principle to an extreme degree. At times he even advanced alone. On one occasion, he single-handedly stormed a machine gun nest and "silenced" a gunner who was threatening his men.

Another knightly quality that shone in Colonel Ripley is disdain for danger. In Vietnam, he earned a reputation for being utterly "fearless." That is not to say that he was foolish, but when circumstances required him to face a perilous situation, he never hesitated.

He saw accepting risk as part of his job as a Marine. He expressed this while speaking to a group of young men considering a career in the Corps. "Risk comes with the job," he told them. "If you are not comfortable with risk, you need to get into a new line of work."

These and many of Colonel Ripley's other qualities are enumerated in *An American Knight*. Thus, I recommend it strongly. I hope my thoughts will help its readers to gain a better appreciation for this Marine who will doubtlessly be remembered as one of the greatest men ever to honor the Corps.

As I said, comparing any modern-day warrior to the mythical knights of the Middle Ages may seem impossible, but if any man fits the bill it is Colonel John Ripley.

Demonstrating this fact in a work as short as *An American Knight* is no easy task, but Mr. Fulkerson took it on and, as far as I am concerned, mission accomplished.

Major General James E. Livingston, USMC (Ret.)
Medal of Honor Recipient
August 31, 2009

PREFACE

Some people have asked me why I decided to write a book about Colonel John Ripley. My answer was simple.

First of all, I felt the need to honor the man. Colonel Ripley was most commonly known for blowing up the Dong Ha Bridge in South Vietnam on Easter Sunday in 1972. What many don't know is that he had already earned legendary status as a warrior during his previous tour in Vietnam as a 26-year-old captain and rifle company commander in 1967. Fewer still are aware of the bold stances he took on cultural issues in America, or the role his Catholic Faith played during his exploits in war. He is, therefore, like a man whose deeds are partially hidden under a veil. I desire to remove that veil for those who might benefit from his example and honor his service to our country and society.

I also decided to write the book because Colonel Ripley is a positive role model which is something desperately lacking in America today. While Americans appreciate the warrior spirit of someone like him, we admire much more a person who is not afraid to tell the truth. General George Patton once said: "America needs some honest men who dare to say what they think, not what they think people want them to think." John Ripley was that man. He was someone who fought for justice on the battlefield as courageously as he defended truth off it, even, and perhaps most especially, when it was inconvenient to do so.

He conducted himself much like a medieval knight. He not only possessed the skills of a warrior, but could temper his aggressive side with wisdom and a truly courteous behavior even in the most extreme circumstances. Throughout his life, he loved the justice, self-sacrifice, honor and loyalty which made up the code of chivalry and observed them throughout his life.

The link between a modern-day Marine and a medieval warrior might seem odd to some, but not to the Marine Corps. In the late eighties, they portrayed the medieval knight as a model in a series of recruiting commercials meant to attract America's youth. Two of these commercials in particular are worthy of mention.

The first portrays a battle on a chessboard between opposing kings dressed in black and white—a good-versus-evil theme that runs throughout the rest of the commercial. The high point occurs when the good knight defeats his nemesis during a medieval clash of swords. Following his victory, the knight approaches the opposing monarch who bows his head in submission.[1] The white knight then rears his horse on its hind legs and, as he raises his sword skyward, it becomes a conductor for a bolt of lightning that transforms the medieval knight into a modern-day Marine. "Maybe you can be one of us..." is the concluding invitation.

The second commercial, more impressive still, begins with a medieval warrior, clad in armor atop a Percheron, bursting through the massive doors of a medieval gothic cathedral. As he proceeds in slow motion to the front of the cathedral, a small boy looks on in awe. The light in his eyes is a clear indicator that he has discovered his life's calling.

Arriving at the front of the cathedral, the knight dismounts and approaches the king. After he kneels on one knee, a clear sign of feudal submission, the king lays a sword on his shoulder. Suddenly, this medieval warrior, who has just been dubbed a knight, is transformed into a modern-day Marine. In both commercials, the audience is left with the unmistakable idea that the knight and the Marine are synonymous and the invitation to be one of *the few, the proud* is irresistible.

Some might find the concept of modern-day American

1. http://www.youtube.com/watch?v=ZjIEZH8VSNM

knighthood too quaint or anachronistic. They might laugh or make a cynical remark upon reading the title. If you are among these, this book is not for you.

It is for those who, seeing the knightly Marine Corps recruiting commercials, would wonder if medieval knighthood were possible in America. It is for those who believe that the spirit of chivalry is not dead and yearn to see living examples of it. It is for the woman who is awed by a man that is willing to fight and, if necessary, die in her defense. In one word, this book is for those Americans who look for someone to show them that their ideals are attainable.

In writing this brief account of the life of Colonel John Ripley, it was not my intent to pen a scholarly work. There will certainly be more extensive biographies about him and I hope to be the first to read them all. Rather, I hoped to express my gratitude, admiration and undying respect for this true American hero.

INTRODUCTION

To a large extent, each of us is the sum of our experiences. Those events and observations teach us about ourselves and shape who we are. We learn from those occurrences, both positive and negative, and they shape our character. Some people faced with difficult experiences, lack the courage to take advantage of them to better themselves. They know only themselves and their personal needs, rendering them incapable of being selfless and noble.

Others know and understand themselves better. They take each experience, measure it, learn from it and use it to build their character. They develop principles that govern and guide them. This was especially true of John Ripley. He nurtured a unique self-awareness and introspection that always led him to make the most of life's lessons and never miss an opportunity to take advantage of what happened around him to better himself.

John Ripley also maintained an incredible focus and drive. Once he set his mind to a task or cause, he did not equivocate or question his decisions. He was not plagued by doubt or hesitation. Each task he undertook, whether it meant performing remarkable actions during the Easter Offensive in 1972 or teaching his children, was completed no matter how difficult or demanding.

These characteristics guided him through a most remarkable life as a combat leader of Marines, academic, husband, father and man of Faith. He showed energy and passion in everything that he did. His self-discipline and sense of duty drove him to block out all distractions in the way of accomplishing whatever mission he was given. The result was a life of singular achievements on the battlefield, in academia and as the head of a family.

Not surprisingly, this man of character and accomplishment

was a man of bedrock Faith. The Church played an instrumental part in his life, underpinned his decisions, and was woven into everything that he did. He understood that there was a Power greater than himself.

In difficult times, when determination and knowledge weren't enough, it was the Faith that carried him through. While many turn to religion simply to rescue them in their darkest times, John Ripley relied on his Faith to strengthen him in doing the things he knew were right. It provided him a quiet confidence that made him unflappable. While he was passionate and determined he was not emotional. In the most chaotic of situations, he maintained a quiet sense of purpose and dignity and an unwavering moral compass.

His experiences and insight showed him the path he had to take; his Faith gave him the courage to take it. This was important since the ways he chose were not always easy. His stances on women in combat and homosexuals in the military were incredibly unpopular and certainly damaging to his career. While his peers may have agreed fully with his positions, few, if any, had the courage to express them.

He was in the vanguard of the culture wars with individuals and groups like the American Society for the Defense of Tradition, Family and Property, who took unpopular stands against the erosion of traditional moral values. His views were as uncomplicated as they were uncompromising.

However, this book illustrates that John Ripley was also devoted to his family. He and his wife formed an unbeatable team and, except in instances when his duty to country called, his family was his greatest priority. Until his death, he remained an engaged parent and grandparent providing his descendents with equal measures of guidance and support. This book provides insights into his role as a father and husband and shows how he lived his Faith, making him an example to his family.

In this, the book is unique. Many have written about John Ripley's exploits on the battlefield and about his thirty-five years as a Marine leader. His maxims on leadership are well documented and timeless. His extraordinary heroism and the events that led to his being awarded the Navy Cross in 1972 are the stuff of Marine Corps legend.

This book does not attempt to revisit the tactics of previous battles. Instead it explores, explains and highlights the accomplishments of this remarkable man in the light of his religion. It provides the chronology of his life experiences and explains the development of his Faith from the time when he was a small boy growing up in a rural southern Virginia town until he became a man engaged in some of the most hotly-debated social issues of his times.

Throughout it all, John Ripley's Faith was the Catholic religion, which he embraced from childhood. In this, he had strong role models in his parents and grandparents. They provided indelible examples of faith and devotion on which he patterned his life. Inspired by them, he practiced Catholicism with the same determination and discipline with which he trained himself physically and academically.

Thus, *An American Knight* uncovers the source of John Ripley's courage and nobility. It answers, in part, why some men, when faced with the impossible, do their duty, while others lack the courage and conviction to seize the moment. After all, a man can be trained physically and mentally to perform a task. However, seeing that task through when tens of thousands flee around you and it seems certain your actions will make your wife a widow and your children orphans takes courage that can only be born of Faith.

Stephen Ripley,
Colonel John Ripley's oldest son
September 12, 2009

Chapter 1
BIRTH AND CHILDHOOD

"Every man dies. Not every man really lives."
— **Unknown**

It was evident at the time of his birth on June 29, 1939, that John Walter Ripley's life would not be easy. Francis and Verna Ripley were living in Keystone, West Virginia and no sooner had they arrived home with their newborn when he had to be rushed back to the hospital because of an illness that almost took his life. Although no one remembers what the ailment was, it seemed appropriate that a man, who would endure every imaginable hardship on the battlefield, should begin his life with a struggle.

This natal fight in no way dampened his vivacious spirit, and his fight for life might have been what led his father to give him the nickname "Baby Buck." Coupled with his rambunctious nature, the image of a wild horse immediately comes to mind with this fatherly pet name.

Francis Droit Ripley was described by those who knew him as possessing one of those unique personalities that are so lamentably rare in the modern world. He was seldom seen without a cigar in his mouth and then, only temporarily for Sunday Mass, which he never missed. The presence of this cigar and his gruff, straightforward way of being earned him several nicknames of his own. The one he most disliked was *FDR* and the one that most fit him was *Bulldog*. Most people just called him Bud, a name so frequently used that his own grandchildren often inquired what his real name was.

Bud Ripley was keenly aware that his ancestors had fought in every American conflict since the Revolutionary War, including some who fought on different sides of the Civil War. There was something distinctly military about him, although his own military aspirations were cut short when he, much to his father's chagrin, was expelled from the United States Naval Academy. It was not because of poor grades. In fact, his younger brother Louis, who went on to become a renowned orthopedic surgeon, considered him to be one of the most intelligent men he knew.

Bud's expulsion occurred because of his curious nature. As a midshipman serving in the fleet, he went to visit a volcano while his ship was docked in Hawaii. As he was returning from his excursion, he realized that he had missed the boat—both figuratively and literally—and along with it the chance to be a commissioned officer. This lost opportunity left its mark on Bud Ripley and from that point forward, he always carried himself as a military man. He was well-groomed, well spoken and, above all, disciplined.

After this disappointing affair, he followed in the footsteps of his father, Walter Starr Ripley, and pursued a career with the railroad, became a mechanical engineer and later manager for the Norfolk & Western (N&W). He was determined, however, that his sons would not make the same mistake he had and cultivated in them the virtues so important for a military career. Foremost among them were a fanatical drive never to waste an opportunity, the tenacity to never quit and diligence in one's duty.

This same spirit of determination is what must have animated "Baby Buck" one day as he crawled across the living room floor. He was only eighteen months old at the time, yet he approached the family sofa with a look of resolve that became so much a part of his personality. When he reached the sofa, he pulled himself up to a standing position and then attempted, with great effort, to climb onto the couch, but his little legs were unable to fulfill the task. Verna was moved by the scene and approached in order to help. Francis Droit stopped her cold in her tracks.

"No, don't help him, let him do it on his own," he said, taking the ever-present cigar from his mouth. "He will learn." After several attempts, "Baby Buck" did in fact achieve his goal and was no worse for the effort. It was a valuable lesson in perseverance.

When it came to raising the children, the Ripleys always worked together harmoniously in spite of the differences in their upbringings.

SOUTHERN INFLUENCE

Francis Droit Ripley was a Yankee from Decatur, Illinois and Verna Holt was a Southern belle from Brookneal, Virginia. He was a fiercely devout Catholic and she was Protestant. A more unlikely pair would be hard to find. Before she ever met Francis Ripley, Verna had said she would never marry a man who was a Republican, a Catholic or a cigar smoker. She ended up getting all three in Bud. Although the marriage did not seem to be a match made in heaven, it did work and the blending of these two personalities played an interesting role in the formation of John Ripley.

Verna was a beautiful woman with a sweet Southern disposition, but she was also described by those who knew her as "the most misunderstood person in the world." This might have been because she saw life through a different prism. Although she did not have a great deal of formal education, she loved reading Shakespeare and had a poetic nature. Besides being a gracious lady with a wonderful sense of humor and constant smile on her face, she was also one to forcefully speak her mind on important matters. Her words of wisdom were often discarded by people who, years later, were forced to admit, "Verna was right."

One such issue inside the Ripley household was the Civil

War. She took a special pride in the fact that her great grandfather, Charles Calvin Holt, fought for the Confederacy with Captain Fry's company in the Virginia Light Artillery and never missed an opportunity to remind her husband that the South really won that war. It is not likely that Bud resisted her on this point, since her contentious side was only skin deep, whereas the gentility of her Southern heritage and good manners went directly to the bone.

Visitors to the Ripley home had the chance to experience her Southern ways firsthand. Those staying overnight were treated, not only to her delicious cooking, but also to a refreshing glass of orange juice in bed upon rising the next day. Her children received the same kind treatment, but when they were ill they had to endure some castor oil thrown in for good measure.

"She was heaven on earth when you were sick," said her eldest child and the only living member of the family, Mary Susan Goodykoontz. The first thing she would do was give the ailing person a "bath in bed."

"Baby Buck" must have relished this, since he loved nothing more than to be clean. This desire for cleanliness stayed with him throughout his life. Once when in high school, he fell off a truck, was knocked unconscious and had to be rushed to the hospital. While those around him feared for his life, his only preoccupation was for his mother to give him a sponge bath.

"He didn't care whether he lived or died," said Mary Susan, "he just wanted to be clean."

POTENTIAL FOR GOOD OR BAD

With the passage of time memories fade, but there was one thing about the youthful John Ripley which stood out in Mary Susan's mind. It was a childhood scene that she could never forget. Christmas was financially difficult in their home. The children learned to make do with whatever gifts they received, which was usually not much.

However, one thing John and his older brother Michael always got was story time with their mother. On Christmas Eve, she would take one of them under each arm while sitting in the family's Morris chair and read aloud Clement Moore's story, '*Twas the Night Before Christmas.*' It was a family tradition which Mary Susan witnessed as a teenager, a scene so special, she recalled, "I never forgot it."

"Our friends would come to the house just to see our mother do this," she said. "They marveled at that, and even now, after so many years, people who witnessed it in their youth say it is what they remember most about our family." Such treatment cultivated a sense of the marvelous in "Baby Buck" which matched his unique gaze. While he inherited his mother's good looks, his most noteworthy facial characteristics were his eyes.

"He had little boy eyes that danced with a sense of wonder," Mary Susan said, "and ones that seemed to communicate an enormous energy and mischief bottled up inside." His eyes also transmitted what she called a "devil may care," or reckless look of one who was thinking about what he would do next. She did not hesitate to point out that he was a rascal who was always "playing tricks on people."

Verna gave a glimpse of this side of her son when he was only seven. She wrote in a letter how "Baby Buck" informed the family one evening what he was going to be in a Halloween play at school. His older brother Michael asked, "And what will you be, a black cat maybe?" "Baby Buck" responded with a smile, "No boy! I'm a big ghost without a head and I scare people half to death with a sheet."

It was clear at this time in his life that he had the potential for good as well as bad. One can only imagine what direction he might have taken, if it weren't for the pious influence of his father, the maternal care of his mother and matriarchal influence of his paternal grandmother Pauline.

Chapter 2
"CULTURE AND REFINEMENT PERSONIFIED"

"Sweet mercy is nobility's true badge."
— **William Shakespeare**

To the degree that Verna contributed to the cultural environment of the household, Bud was, without a doubt, the one who set the religious tone. This was due to his mother Pauline Droit. Although he inherited a martial side from his father's Polish ancestors, his mother's French lineage was the foundation of his strong religious convictions.

She possessed a strong Faith and did everything in her power to pass her beliefs on to everyone with whom she came into contact, but most especially to her progeny. Her devotion to the Blessed Mother was evident from the regularity with which she prayed the rosary. She also showed this dedication by continuing the family tradition of naming one daughter in each family Mary.

Her devotion to the Crucified Savior was equally intense. Besides observing the Good Friday fast, she imposed absolute silence upon herself in remembrance of the sufferings of Our Lord. Such strictness made for humorous family anecdotes which have been handed down through the years. Most amusing among them was the frustration Pauline had in attempting non-verbal communication with the maid. She was reduced to hand gestures and written notes, but would not permit a word to leave her mouth as she, in monk-like fashion, reflected on the sacrifices of Our Lord.

Her Eucharistic devotion was equally fervent and observed with military precision. Every morning, she was up before the crack of dawn in preparation for her daily reception of Holy Communion. She then walked to the local church at 6:15 a.m., where Bud and her other sons would serve Mass. Her love for the Church showed through in a letter she wrote to her daughter-in-law after Verna announced her plans to convert.

December 8, 1936

Verna,

My own little daughter, as much so as anyone could be and not be my very own blood. I was too full for words when you told me that blessed news Friday night. My prayers have been for you every morning and night since you came into our family regardless of where you were or what you were doing. Our Blessed Mother and Saint Ann have been so good to me in listening to my prayers for you and yours. You are an angel in the sight of heaven and may God always keep you that way. Life's rough spots will seem smoother to you now. Fathers Gelsemian and Hoffuer were here to dinner last night and rejoiced with me. We made a novena in honor of the Immaculate Conception…You chose a beautiful feast day [the Immaculate Conception] to join the Church, the day of all innocence. God bless you, and all those dear to you will continue to be in my prayers as long as I live.

Mother

Her spiritual life and matriarchal influence were felt well beyond the family hearth and led everyone in town, no matter what their religious affiliation was, to call her Mother Ripley. She earned this affectionate epithet by numerous spiritual and corporal works of mercy which included everything from visiting prisoners at the local jail to helping the homeless—the more destitute the better.

Some referred to her as a "crusader for good" because she led the way while others stood by with their arms crossed. Mary Susan aptly defined her as "culture and refinement personified." She was a person capable of entertaining the Queen of England with the same ease as a destitute hobo.

"The concept which most comes to mind when remembering her," she continued, "was noblesse oblige, because she went beyond preaching and embodied the principles to which she adhered." Although she inherited a fortune from her father who owned valuable property in southern Illinois, the money in her pocket could in no way match the value of the gold in her heart.

"Baby Buck" had the chance to observe closely the admirable harmony of these qualities in the soul of his grandmother when he was still just a boy. Due to financial hardships, he was sent to live with his grandparents temporarily. During this time, Pauline prepared him for his First Communion as only she could do.

CATHOLIC PRACTICES

Pauline died some years later when "Baby Buck" was only ten, but Bud would continue to exercise as strong a religious influence within the family as his mother had. Like her, he had a great devotion to the Blessed Mother. Mary Susan said he was "addicted to the rosary."

At noon every day, the family would pray the rosary and it didn't matter who was there or what they were doing. This was usually prayed in the parlor where a crucifix hung above the mantle with a candle on both sides. On either side of the candles was a picture, one of General Robert E. Lee and the other of General Stonewall Jackson. It was, perhaps, the family's way of combining Verna's Southern heritage with Bud's Catholic Faith.

Seeing their father on his knees in prayer made a great impression on Bud's children. This was a very important factor in his sons' development, since religion has often been erroneously presented as something only for ladies. In the Ripley household, the men not only practiced their religion, but often played a leading role. Once, while they were saying the family rosary, John Walter began pacing the floor in a perturbed way. His sisters were "multitasking" when they should have been focused on the mysteries.

"He didn't approve of us sewing, knitting and embroidering, while we were supposed to be praying the rosary," said Mary Susan. After reaching a boiling point, John Walter interrupted the rosary with an amusing request that was full of biting wit, "Anyone for tennis?" Since his siblings figured it was okay to do anything else when they should have been praying, he figured why not suggest some outdoor activity. In spite of being the youngest in the family, they got the message.

"He did not want us to do anything," she said, "while the rosary was going on. So we stopped right then and there."

He undoubtedly inherited this seriousness in practicing the Faith from his grandmother Pauline and his father. While Bud loved the Catholic Faith, he didn't go along with the liturgical changes of the sixties. In a position of resistance, he would obstinately follow the Mass by saying his prayers in Latin out loud for everyone to hear. The priest finally had enough and asked him to go to the back of the church if he was going to pray in Latin. He acquiesced, but continued to pray his prayers, as remembered by a grandchild, "uncomfortably loud." He made such a mark on the parish priest, however, that the latter made a concession upon Bud's death and said some of the prayers at his funeral in Latin.

At the time of John Walter's birth, the Ripleys were one of the few Catholic families in Keystone. They did not have the luxury of a parish church and were resigned to travel to the nearby city of Vivian to attend Mass at a tiny mission church. During the winter months, the Ripley family arrived exceptionally early to give Bud time to fire up the potbelly stove so that the Church would be warm for Mass. The congregation was so small, that if it weren't for the Ripley family, there would have been no Mass on Holy Days.

"We would often go to the priest's home," said Mary Susan, "and get him out of bed to remind him that it was a Holy Day and ask him to say Mass. It was a treat for us," she continued, "because we got to go to a restaurant afterwards before returning to school."

Mary Susan studied with the nuns in Nazareth, Kentucky and took a great pride in her Catholic formation. Since the family often relied on a traveling priest for Mass and religious formation, teaching catechism to the boys often fell on her shoulders. She, and her sister Patricia, would sometimes torment their brothers for their lack of knowledge regarding the truths of the Faith. They did not think George, the second oldest in the family, was holy enough because he "didn't know the definition of mortal sin, the seven sacraments or the gifts of the Holy Spirit and because he didn't take philosophy."

John Walter was a particularly dismal student, although he did seem to take some advantage of the religious formation he received while the family lived in Portsmouth, Ohio. They moved there when he was five years old and for two years the Franciscan nuns at Holy Redeemer parochial school taught him. Like his brothers, he did not learn all the subjects he should have, but he did absorb the memorable things which the nuns taught him about the angels.

While instructing their pupils about the celestial hosts, the nuns told the wide-eyed students to make sure to leave part of the seat vacant for their guardian angels. When relating this fact at the end of his life, he chuckled at the thought of the students in the classroom sitting on half a seat to leave room for their personal angels.

The Ripleys moved to Radford, Virginia in 1947, where Catholics were in such a minority that Mass was said in the tiny American Legion hall by a missionary priest. While some people questioned Bud's wisdom in making such a move, Mary Susan remembers her father being enthusiastic about going "into territory where he could proselytize." When his friends pointed out that there were no Catholics in Radford, Bud Ripley simply responded with apostolic zeal, "That is why I want to go there."

It is not known if the Ripley boys shared Bud's love for souls, but they did share the responsibilities. They were assigned the disagreeable task of cleaning the hall before Mass. This entailed picking up all the beer bottles after Saturday night parties. They would then gather as many old newspapers as they could find to absorb the puddles of beer so the faithful could have a dry spot to kneel. Some parishioners had rubber mats to pad their knees, but not the Ripleys. Bud's children were all raised to live a life based on principle. Since they were accustomed to less than ideal conditions for the observance of their Sunday obligation, kneeling on the floor would be a minor inconvenience. It was also a valuable lesson regarding the hardships of life which must be endured with patience.

They finally got their own church in 1952 and, by then, both John and Michael were old enough to serve Mass. Bud took it upon himself to teach them their prayers in Latin.

By then, John Walter was becoming an energetic young man. Although he believed in angels and served Mass as a boy, he was neither a cherub nor a little choir boy. He was quickly becoming a little man with a penchant for mischief that earned him another nickname, Huckleberry Finn.

Chapter 3
HUCKLEBERRY FINN

On the fields of friendly strife are sown the
seeds that on other days and other fields
will bear the fruits of victory.
—General Douglas MacArthur

When the family arrived in Radford, they moved into a house owned by the N&W Railroad which they rented for some years before purchasing. It had a name emblazoned in beveled glass on the front door. It was called *Castleton* after the former mayor of Radford.

The location of the house could not have been more appropriate for a boy like John Walter who loved the outdoors. Outside their backdoor was Castle Island in the middle of the New River. A stone's throw upstream was a railroad bridge with tracks that abruptly ended on the opposite bank earning it the name, "bridge to nowhere." The family simply referred to it as "the trestle." That bridge became the central element in the maturing process of Radford's "Huckleberry Finn." He spent half his life on top of, underneath or around it, and the stories of his antics are almost endless.

BATTLE OF CLOYD'S MOUNTAIN
What is most ironic about his carefree boyhood is an obscure piece of Civil War history that the Ripley family knew by heart.

It was a battle that began on May 9, 1864 at the foot of Cloyd's Mountain, just west of downtown Radford, and was part of Ulysses S. Grant's spring offensive. Of the roughly 9,000 soldiers that were involved on both sides, over 1,500 were casualties. The Confederate Army under Brigadier General Albert Jenkins had fewer than 3,000 men and lost a full 23% of his entire force in a battle which ended up in hand-to-hand combat. As things worsened, the Confederate Army tried to retreat to the nearby city of Christiansburg where they could regroup and make a stand on the following day. The Northern army caught up with them in the city of Radford.

Since the Ingles Ferry Bridge, three miles up the road from the city, had already been burned, the only way for the Northerners to cross the New River was by way of the railroad bridge in downtown Radford. Everything focused on that bridge as North and South began a cannon duel from opposite sides of the river.

Unable to resist over 3-to-1 odds, the Southern forces were faced with a perplexing dilemma. The bridge needed to go, but by destroying it, they would cut themselves off from much-needed supplies. If the North crossed that bridge, however, they would have no hopes of resistance. Southern forces eventually decided to burn down the bridge. The events of that battle provided an eerie foreshadowing of John Ripley's future actions.

MARION "MICKEY" RUNION

The railroad trestle outside the Ripley home was a short distance down the road from where those Southern forces fought the Radford battle. It provided a thoughtful view when seen from the vantage point of Castle Island where John Walter spent a large part of his youth with his best friend Marion Runion—so much time that Verna swore half of her silverware was probably on that island.

Marion or "Mickey" as he was called, was the type of friend one would expect John Ripley to choose since both shared the same qualities of soul. Mickey was from a staunchly Baptist family, however, and tried on numerous occasions to get his best friend to attend Bible lessons on Sundays. Although Bud never allowed John Walter to attend, Mickey could not help but admire his principled stand. Both young men were fearless and ended up choosing similar paths in life. Whereas John Ripley chose the Marine Corps, Mickey went on to serve as an Army dentist, and died a tragic death in Vietnam when he volunteered to go on a mission of mercy. The helicopter in which he was riding was brought down by enemy fire and exploded when it hit the ground, killing everyone on board.[1]

From the moment they met, the two were inseparable. It is not a matter of public record what they spoke about during the quiet evenings on Castle Island. It would be natural to think that some of their conversations drifted toward the history of the region and the striking similarity between "the trestle" in front of them and the one strategically destroyed by fellow Southerners a century before. Both of them identified with the South and John had heard the epic stories from his mother of the underdog region fighting against superior odds. Cloyd's Mountain was simply one chapter in Civil War history, while "the trestle" in front of them represented a constant reminder of the perils of war.

TRESTLE TREATMENT

John Ripley loved challenges and it would be easy to see him sitting around the campfire remembering the Battle of Cloyd's Mountain and imagining himself in the shoes of those Confederate heroes in their desperate struggle so many years before. He wasn't much into reading, but did appreciate the military deeds of his ancestors and loved pulling off acts of daring. Most of these involved the trestle. His favorite stunt, which fascinated his nephews, was when he would hand-walk, arm over arm, across the bottom of the bridge like

---

1. Mickey was buried near the city of Blacksburg, Virginia, and until his own death, John Ripley never went home for a visit without decorating his friend's grave with flowers.

a kid playing on monkey bars. This was an alarming feat when one considers that he was dangling from the dizzying height of nearly 40 feet from the river below. It was not long before his nephews were lining up for what they called the "trestle treatment."

They did not hesitate when he suggested they conquer their fears by walking across the top of the bridge. Although there was no real danger involved, the height was frightening. This became known in the Ripley family as the "rite of passage"— an initiation for every little nephew. However, nieces were not included. Although they loved Uncle John and considered it a privilege just to be with him, they may have resented not being part of the fun. Nevertheless, he would never subject the girls to such treatment.

Because of his upbeat personality, he formed lasting friendships with most everyone he met. Another one of his friends, or "partners in crime," was Danny Jett who also served in Vietnam and today lives in Radford. The two of them, along with Mickey Runion, became known as the "River Rats" because of the amount of time they spent around the water. Danny Jett was incapable of restraining a smile as he reflected on some of their escapades.

While not one of the River Rats, Louis Semones was a friend whose father was a dentist in town. Louis would frequently get a hold of his father's appointment pad and write bogus dentist visits to get his friends out of classes. It worked really well until the three of them decided to have a doctor's appointment on the same day. Coach Jim Painter, the acting principal that day, was also their football coach. He knew their frequent visits to the dentist were suspect, but when they all turned up absent, he saw right through it. They were duly punished, but it did nothing to dampen the adventuresome spirit of John, the obvious ring-leader of the group.

LIVING LIFE ON THE EDGE

Like most American boys, John Walter had a fascination for anything that explodes. His favorite pastime was taking glass jars full of gasoline across the river with Danny Jett. After lighting a small fire underneath them, they returned to the opposite bank and used them for target practice with their .22 rifles. This not only developed their shooting skills but when they hit the target, they would take an enormous delight in the explosion it caused. In a town of 9,000, this created quite a stir and inevitably they would hear the sound of sirens, forcing them to hide until the coast was clear. Escape was not difficult since they knew the countryside like the backs of their hands.

When they weren't blowing something up, they were also known to make unauthorized visits to Harry McGuire's strawberry patch. It was for this reason that Mr. McGuire was often seen snoring away on his front porch with his shotgun strategically laid across his lap. He knew the River Rats had a sweet tooth and kept his gun loaded to keep them honest. On one occasion, Danny Jett remembers them lying in the middle of the patch eating to their heart's content when Mr. McGuire woke up. It was one of the rare occasions when they were unable to escape unscathed. However, being shot with rock salt did not bother John Walter who had a high tolerance for pain.

He also took a genuine thrill in accomplishing things which others were unwilling to attempt. This is what most likely fascinated him about snakes which he took special delight in catching and showing off as trophies to his friends. The best place to find them was on the banks of the New River, where the larger black snakes would sun themselves as they slept.

"These trophies ended up in places where they weren't supposed to," said Mr. Jett. He tells the story of how John found a black snake one day that was so big it took the help of both him and Mickey to carry it up the bank. Before arriving at the top,

John Walter had already figured out a good use for it. The three of them made their way to the tie yard. They quietly approached the guardhouse which he described as being no bigger than an outhouse. The guard was inside taking an afternoon nap with his feet propped up on the desk, not realizing he was about to be the victim of a terrifying prank. As he soundly slept, Danny Jett opened the door, while Mickey Runion and John tossed the snake onto the chest of the sleeping watchman. The commotion was enough to wake him and the sight of a snake crawling down his leg almost gave him a heart attack. He nearly tore the building down trying to get out of it which gave the pranksters ample time to escape.

Mr. Jett recalled, on another occasion, how John's attempt to catch a snake without a stick was unsuccessful. He was subsequently bitten and his hand swelled up for two weeks, but that didn't bother him either. Not too much did. He just liked living life on the edge and the ease with which he got into trouble was only matched by his ability to get out of it. With his ever-present smile and agreeable demeanor, he disarmed people who would have normally been irate over his shenanigans. Marie Dobyns knew this all too well. She taught him choir when he attended Radford High School and today lives in New Castle, Virginia.

"If there was something going on," she said, "you could take one look at John and just knew it was him. He was a little imp," she continued, "but I loved him."

Chapter 4
CITY OF RADFORD

*A love for tradition has never weakened
a nation, indeed it has strengthened
nations in their hour of peril.*
— **Sir Winston Churchill**

The cultural environment of Radford played as important a role in John's formation as anything. The world in which he grew up was radically different from today. This helps explain the decisions he made in later life. Marie Dobyns described the time period as the "nearest thing to heaven that I will ever experience, until I get there. Everybody's word was their bond," she said, "and you could depend on people."

The remnants of the spirit of that time still linger in the air. It can be seen in the remaining members of the "greatest generation," like Robert Lowman who, to this day, exercises a stable and respectable influence in the city. He practices law and described how the behavior of most people in the fifties was based on an unpublished code of conduct.

"You just knew what was the right thing to do," he said. "We can quote laws all day long, but you and I know what is right. We have 37,000 statutes," he continued, pointing to the bookshelf behind him, "but there are just ten basic rules. What else would you need?"

At that time, the city had only one co-ed high school and one all-girls college. The boys from the city were allowed to date the girls at the college, but only if Dr. Mary Ledge Moffett approved. A group of men from that time still gather for a morning coffee at Wade's Grocery Store in downtown Radford where they "solve the problems of the world." They all remembered Dr. Moffett well. Besides being the dean of students, they said she also authored a book on marriage and the family, which the locals found quite amusing since she was never married. She ran the school "like Joseph Stalin ran Russia," they all were quick to say.

CUSTOMS OF THE TIME

Nowhere are the cultural differences of those days so apparent as in the manner with which she watched over her girls. To start with, you could not even go out with a girl from the college until you endured an interview with Dr. Moffett. She had to see if you were appropriate for the young lady. If approved, the parents would have to send a letter two weeks prior to the date, in order for their son to obtain formal permission.

Jim Graham knew the procedure quite well. He was John's classmate in high school and knew Dr. Moffett. Since he dated some of the girls, he was subjected to the interviews. Once the authorization was acquired, he explained, Dr. Moffett would only allow the couple to walk to the local theater in town. They never were allowed to ride in a car by themselves. They would then have to be back at the school in observance of a strict 9:30 p.m. curfew. The couple was allowed to visit a while longer on the screened-in front porch, but only under adult supervision. They were not allowed to leave that porch.

Dress codes were also different then. The young men had to wear a coat and tie and, whenever the girls went downtown, they had to be clothed properly in a dress. On Sunday, this included a hat and white gloves.

One cannot help but contrast Dr. Moffett's rules for dating with the modern-day custom of "hooking up" and all the emotional roller coaster rides such practices provoke. She was not the equivalent of a Communist dictator, as some portray her to have been, but rather a female Saint Michael the Archangel defending the most precious thing a woman possesses: her integrity.

The memories which the Radford men related about the past are more than mere nostalgic reflections of a bygone era. They are descriptions of the good order and harmony which still existed in that small southwest Virginia town, before the upheavals of the turbulent sixties were unleashed on the world.

This respect for women, which is so lost in today's world, must have had a great influence on John Ripley. Images of white-gloved young ladies going on a Sunday stroll with beautiful hats matched the idea of femininity he developed observing his mother, while the rules governing proper conduct were exactly those of his grandmother Pauline.

NO BETTER FRIEND, NO WORSE ENEMY

Although society has changed a lot since then, Jim Graham remembers very well another incident from that time. It occurred one evening in the summer of 1957, when he and his brother were on a date with some girls from the college. As they were making their way home to meet Dr. Moffett's curfew, they saw an all-too-familiar scene. A group of boys from the nearby city of Parrot was standing in front of the local pool hall. It was common for the young men from that coal-mining town to visit Radford for an evening of fun that often degenerated into fistfights with the local boys. As expected, the Parrot boys blocked their way and disrespected the young ladies in hopes of starting something. John Ripley and Mickey Runion just happened to walk by when the scene unfolded.

The code of conduct for those in Radford regarding the girls of the college was crystal clear. The Radford boys, John Ripley included, were no saints, but there was a limit to their mischief and the Parrot boys had simply crossed the line. Furthermore, there were four of them against Jim and his brother, a numerical difference that John Ripley's sense of justice would simply not allow to go unpunished. He did not appreciate bullies,

especially those that were taking advantage of superior numbers to throw their weight around. Since John Ripley was the
type to always side with the underdog, this was the wrong
night for the Parrot gang to pick a fight.

"What's going on here?" he asked. This was no doubt a
rhetorical question. All the Radford boys knew that the members of the Parrott gang were troublemakers.

"These guys are harassing us," Jim responded. As he
explained their predicament, the Parrot boys continued to
block the sidewalk, not realizing the fight they had just bought.
Jim Graham described the ever-present smile on John's face
very well.

"It was the type of smile which said he had either just done
something or he was about to do something." In this case, it
was the latter.

"Don't worry about it," John said, "We'll take care of it." In
spite of being outnumbered, John and Mickey forced the out-
siders into an alley and gave all of them a beating they would
not soon forget.

Such stories might convey the wrong idea of John Ripley.
He was not just about fighting and mischief, but if a fight came
knocking at his door he wasn't one to shy away from it. He
also possessed a fierce loyalty and refused to sit idly by when
close friends needed his help. In this way, from an early age,
he embodied a slogan, popularized in the Marine Corps by
General James Mattis, "no better friend, no worse enemy."

There was, however, another side of the young man which
was seen more frequently in the inner sanctum of the Ripley
home, where he loved to sing and lived life to its fullest.

Chapter 5
HEARING THE BATTLE CRY

Accept the challenges so that you can
feel the exhilaration of victory.
— **General George Patton**

In spite of not being from a higher class in society, the Ripleys were looked upon as models in the community because of their strong religious convictions and patriotism. They had a fierce love of country and were proud of the fact that all their sons would go on to serve the nation loyally.

Their home was an attractive place to spend the evening and became a hub of activity for family members and friends. All of the children were musically talented, with the exception of John Walter. The only things he knew how to play were his vocal chords which he exercised to their fullest. He simply loved to sing and was always a central figure in family get-togethers. Music was an integral part of family life, creating a joyful atmosphere which contributed to the upbeat attitude John Walter would maintain throughout his life. He was rarely seen without a smile on his face, even in the midst of his greatest sufferings.

The evening program at the Ripley home always entailed the family rosary after dinner, followed by music. Bud usually occupied a side chair where he would sit with a lapboard and three-ring binder, writing down his thoughts for a book about World War II. While Bud was writing, the rest of the family played music, sang and sometimes even danced.

Although they eventually obtained formal musical instruction, the children were first taught music by their mother. Mary Susan recalls how Verna, in spite of not knowing how to play anything, taught her the piano. What Verna lacked in instruction, she made up for with a good ear. She would begin her "lessons" by asking Mary Susan if she knew a certain song. If she didn't, Verna would hum it while her daughter pecked at the keys until she figured it out.

"I would then play it with just one finger," said Mary Susan. "Mother would listen patiently, then say 'now put the chords to it.'" If she got the wrong chord, Verna would tell her and request that she try again. This process would continue until she got it right. Mrs. Goodykoontz boasts of having learned over 150 different songs with her mother's help.

While Verna was giving lessons, Bud, a monotone with no musical talent, would tap his foot to the music as he pondered the battles of World War II. The commotion did not bother him in the least and it was not unusual for him to interrupt his reflections to comment on the melody.

"I don't know anything about music," he would frequently say, "but if you can't tap your foot to it, it's not worth much."

As the years passed, Bud continued to write while Verna instructed and the end results were evenings of irresistible family sing-alongs. Those visiting the home could either join in or entertain themselves with the Ripleys, each of whom possessed a rich personality and unique individuality.

SIBLINGS

Mary Susan, the eldest, became an excellent pianist and during family evenings she, along with her youngest brother, was something of a ringleader. Today she remains an easily recognizable member of the clan who possesses the same grit as her baby brother. At 79 years of age, she boasts of never having used a pillow during her entire life. Such things, she said, are for "sissies" and their father raised them to be tough. She also cited a patriotic reason related to American troops overseas.

"If they can sleep without a pillow in the field," she reasons, "then so can I."

George Holt Ripley, the second oldest, was a distinguished graduate from the Virginia Military Institute (VMI) and a career Marine who retired with the rank of Colonel. He mastered the five-string banjo, but was equally skillful with other instruments.

So was his younger sister Patricia Anne who gravitated towards the clarinet. She graduated from Virginia Tech with a degree in General Science, which in no way describes her intellectual abilities. In fact, she was an expert mathematician whose mind, according to the dean of students, equaled that of the highest engineering student that ever attended Virginia Tech. Her unassuming ways led family members to think she was simply a librarian. It was only after her death from complications due to Alzheimer's that they discovered she was an expert code breaker for the CIA.

Then there was Michael Joseph who could play anything he laid his hands on. While he was playing the clarinet for the Radford High School band, John Walter, fifteen months his junior, was playing guard for the football team. He did not totally understand why his brother chose to play an instrument when he could be hitting someone on the football field with him. The two of them were as opposite as night and day, but in spite of their differences, they were inseparable.

Michael followed George's lead, joined the Marines and distinguished himself as an expert pilot. Upon graduation, his drill instructor paid him what is perhaps the highest honor a Marine can receive. He took off his campaign hat, which symbolizes the Marine Corps, and gave it to the stunned grunt. He eventually went on to serve three thirteen-month tours in Vietnam and was considered by many to be the most tested pilot of his time. When he returned to the United States in 1971, the Marine Corps asked him to test fly the new Harrier jump jet. He died on one of the first runs when his plane crashed into the

Chesapeake Bay. However, he left such a mark on the Marine Corps that each year, the top Marine test pilot in the United States is presented with the *Mike Ripley Award* in his honor.

MAKING OF A MARINE[1]

John Walter never learned to play an instrument, which is not surprising considering the amount of time he spent in the great outdoors. However, what he lacked in musical ability, he made up for with his voice. He sang with an unmatched gusto and especially liked the sing-alongs around the piano with his sister Mary Susan. The songs which most attracted him were those that spoke of true-life tragedies, such as "The Titanic" and the "Wreck of Old 57." The latter described a horrific train wreck in which the conductor was burned alive by boiling water from the locomotive. The way he bellowed out these songs with deep emotion indicated his kindred spirit with individuals caught in perilous circumstances.

The human drama of his favorite songs also fed his yearning for greater things. As he began to mature, this desire only increased and Robert Lowman took advantage of every opportunity to stoke the flames of John Walter's idealism. As a World War II veteran who fought in Okinawa, he had plenty of stories to capture the imagination of Bud's youngest son. His frequent visits to the Ripley home gave Mr. Lowman the chance to recruit the youngest member of the family. John was only twelve at the time, but Mr. Lowman could see the potential for the Marine Corps shining in his eyes. During one of his visits, he gave John a Marine Corps jacket. On other occasions, he would bring Marine Corps emblems for John Walter to put on the jacket.

"Now that's what you ought to be," he would whisper in the

---

1. The facts in the next two sections were put together using research conducted by Richard Botkin but were not included in the final manuscript of his book, *Ride the Thunder*. These facts will forthwith be referenced as an unpublished portion.

boy's ear. "You should be a Marine. Stand up straight," he told the young man. "Be honorable, and respect your fellow man and the Marines. Pick him up if he falls and don't leave anyone behind. We need all the Marines we can get." Thus, the first seeds were planted.

It wasn't long before John Walter got a job selling the local newspaper. At that time, Radford was a stopping point for soldiers and Marines returning from the Korean War who were heading east to Richmond or north to Washington, D.C. John Walter closely analyzed these military men as they departed the train and relished the brief interaction with them while making a sale. This provided him with a chance to examine the different human type of each branch of the Armed Forces. He noticed how the Marines stood out from the rest. They never slouched but always held themselves upright. Besides having a unique professionalism, they also possessed a quiet confidence which others lacked. However, most of all, they walked with a particular swagger he found attractive.

It was not uncommon to see these military men hitchhiking. Bud never failed to give them a lift, even if it meant a detour from his planned route. Having Korean War veterans in the same car gave the impressionable youth more time for close observation. He would listen attentively as his father engaged them in conversation and he absorbed every word of their experiences abroad.

On one occasion, Bud picked up a Marine who was hobbling down the road on crutches. As John Walter looked at the Marine sitting next to him in the back seat, he was shocked to see blood seeping through his trousers. The concern in his eyes was immediately communicated to his father who was watching the scene through the rear view mirror. Bud wasted no time getting the Marine to a local hospital for proper treatment and the manner in which this Marine quietly accepted the pain made a great impact on his son.

FOLLOWING A DREAM

It was around this time that John's oldest brother George graduated from VMI and was commissioned as a 2nd Lieutenant in the Marine Corps. A year later he was home on leave during the Christmas season and brought with him a copy of a book called *Battle Cry*, a novel which graphically described the rigors of boot camp and the adventures of the Pacific war. Somehow, this book ended up in the hands of John Walter. By the time he finished, he knew what he wanted to do with his life.

His dream was to be a Marine like those described in the book. His father thought he would make a fine officer and strongly encouraged him to seek admission to the Naval Academy. Bud was determined that John would fulfill the dream which had eluded him. This would entail the kind of study that John was not used to doing. Up until that time, he had not been a very good student. He preferred to experience life rather than read about it. All of that was about to change when he accepted the challenge to seek an appointment to the Naval Academy. Knowing his disinterest in intellectual endeavors, Bud enrolled John in a prep course to give him a better chance on the entrance exam. His solution for his wild-spirited boy was simple. He locked him in his room for weeks on end and forced him to study.

When it came time for the exam, John Walter took a bus to Wytheville, Virginia, about 30 miles away, to take the test. His scores were sufficient for him to become his congressman's fourth alternate, but not good enough for the class that would graduate in 1961. He would have to wait a year before trying again and decided, at 17 years of age, to join the Marine Corps early. To do so, he would need both parents' permission. His father was overjoyed but Verna wept. However, in the end she acquiesced and signed the papers.

Chapter 6
NAVAL ACADEMY

*Every day you may make progress. Every step
may be fruitful. Yet there will stretch out before
you an ever-lengthening, ever-ascending,
ever-improving path. You know you will never
get to the end of the journey. But this, so
far from discouraging, only adds to the
joy and glory of the climb.*
—**Sir Winston Churchill**

It comes as no surprise that John Ripley mastered the physical side of being a Marine. However, he was about to learn, once again, the hardships of intellectual life. After spending a year in the Marine Corps, he applied once more for an appointment to the Naval Academy and was ultimately accepted. However, his high school grades were so poor that he was forced to spend a year at the Naval Academy Preparatory School (NAPS),[1] then located in Bainbridge, Maryland.

Bud once again locked him in his room for a week and obliged him to study. The Huckleberry Finn existence he so intensely enjoyed during his youth was clearly over. It was now time to force himself to develop his brain as much as he had his brawn. He faced this challenge as seriously as he did everything in life and considered that anything less would be squandering a great opportunity, a mistake he refused to make.

After finishing up at NAPS, he was prepared to enter the hallowed grounds of the United States Naval Academy. It was as much a fulfillment of his father's dream as his own. Bud never let his sons forget his missed opportunity of attending this prestigious institution and John Ripley was naturally

---

1. In July of 2006, the Naval Academy Prep School, now located in Newport, Rhode Island, honored him by naming its new dormitory "Ripley Hall."

happy for having made it.

The night before he was to enter the Academy, he went out with some friends to celebrate the occasion. Later in the evening, the Ripleys were surprised to hear a car horn blowing incessantly. When they went out to see what the problem was, they found John bent over the steering wheel in excruciating pain from what turned out to be appendicitis. He was rushed to the hospital where he underwent an emergency appendectomy. The surgery and recovery time caused him to arrive late at the Academy and served to increase his high degree of apprehension at entering such a school. Although he had made it through NAPS, he knew that he was not a brilliant student and the delay in his arrival only increased his fear of the unknown.

THIRST FOR KNOWLEDGE

It was during his four years at the Academy that he would undergo one of the most extraordinary transformations in his life. His childhood had been anything but model. Although he was sometimes reckless in his behavior and mischievous to a fault, he had always possessed potential for much more that was waiting to flourish. While at the Academy, he recognized an image of what he wanted to be, set his sights on it and never looked back. His application to studies led him to accomplish things in the classroom, he only thought possible on the obstacle course. During his time at the Academy, he acquired the ability to apply himself to study and a thirst for knowledge he maintained for the rest of his life.[2]

While John Ripley worked hard, he found it difficult to

2.   Colonel Ripley wrote many historical articles and essays, contributed to a number of books and was one of the foremost historians on the battle of Iwo Jima. His last post in the Marine Corps was Director for History and Museums. In recognition of his numerous accomplishments, he went on to receive the prestigious Distinguished Graduate Award from the Academy. He was the first Marine to receive that honor.

overcome the academic hole he had dug for himself in his early years. Academics at the Naval Academy were as rigorous as any school in the country and John Ripley was in way over his head. He finished second to last in his class academically, but with some of the highest marks in leadership, physical ability and military aptitude.

Paul Galanti was a classmate of John. He served in Vietnam as a fighter pilot, was shot down, captured and spent seven years in a POW camp. He said John Ripley was like any other student except for his good study habits which he continued to develop even after leaving the academy.

"During deployments, while others were out partying," he said, "John was usually reading books and virtually became a philosopher."

Years later, John Ripley reflected on what he learned at the Naval Academy which became for him true lessons of life, such as the ability to fight and survive against overwhelming odds. The rigors of intellectual life he likened to future battles where he was forced to endure "incessant combat with virtually no hope of reinforcement, and to never accept the odds as being actually overwhelming." Perhaps, the most valuable lesson he learned had to do with mental endurance, which he defined as: "an attitude that your mind imposes over your physical limitations." He continued, "These limitations are real but are referred to in the Marine Corps as luxuries. You are not permitted to have physical limitations. We don't issue those [in the Marine Corps]."[3]

His ability to push himself came in handy during a mishap that occurred in December of 1961. He was to graduate in June and, while home on vacation, he borrowed George's car for a

3. Comments made during lectures Colonel Ripley gave at the headquarters of the American Society for the Defense of Tradition, Family and Property (TFP) in Spring Grove, Pennsylvania. Hereafter referred to as TFP lectures.

night out on the town. An enjoyable evening turned bad in a
hurry. On the drive home, he missed a stop sign and plowed
head-on into an embankment. The impact was so violent that
he was thrown head first through the windshield which gashed
his forehead open causing a stream of blood to run down his
face. With no one in sight, he kept his presence of mind and
walked to a nearby house to get help. His countenance was so
disfigured, however, that it produced more fear than sympathy
among the occupants who refused him assistance. Exasperated
by their lack of compassion, he went elsewhere and finally got
help and a ride to the local hospital.

He bounced back from this setback with nothing more serious than a bruised ego.

Six months later, graduation day came and certainly every
midshipman was contemplating the thirty days' leave to which
all were entitled before their next assignment; every student
with the exception of now 2nd Lieutenant John Ripley. No
sooner had his graduation cap hit the ground, than he was
preparing himself psychologically for the next phase of his life
as a Marine. Two days later, after bypassing the break, he
reported to the Basic School for Marine Officers in Quantico,
Virginia. He was the only midshipman to do so.

FROM *DOUBLE TROUBLE* TO *TRIPLE THREAT*

In May of 1964, he was sent to Fort Benning for three weeks'
training with the Army's Airborne School. A short time later,
his unit was training in the Mediterranean. Their return trip
took them through Portugal where he had an unexpected
encounter with the commanding officer of 2nd Force
Reconnaissance Company. Seeing John Ripley's airborne
wings, the officer invited him to become a part of Force Recon,
an elite group within the Marine Corps given the most difficult
missions of deep reconnaissance and direct action that never

reach the front pages. This group of warriors was originally founded during World War II as an amphibious reconnaissance battalion. For years, they were used primarily for gathering information deep behind enemy lines. In 1957, the year John Ripley enlisted in the Corps, they saw their first military action in Vietnam.

He did not hesitate when invited to be part of these elite warriors and quickly completed the Jumpmaster course and US Navy SCUBA, or Under Water Demolition (UDT) program.[4] By doing so, he earned the in-house distinction among Force Recon members of being dubbed *double trouble*. He then went on to complete the U.S. Army Ranger course.

"In our training," he said about the Ranger program, "we were kept in a constantly deprived state; sleep deprivation all the time, and even [deprivation of] food. They did that purposely, and it had a very good effect, because you learned you could operate under these conditions when your body was weak and your mind was addled."[5]

Out of the 150 soldiers and Marines who started the training, only half finished. Among the three honor graduates was 2nd Lieutenant John Ripley.[6]

With his graduation in May of 1965, his degree of danger to anyone who got in his way was upgraded from *double trouble* to *triple threat*.

After receiving his new Ranger tab, he quickly saw his first action when he was deployed, in May of 1965, to the Dominican Republic to quell a political crisis created by locals who were influenced by the Communist revolution

---

4. UDT was the precursor of the modern day Navy SEALs.
5. http://www.mca-Marines.org/Leatherneck/sep08-Marine-inducted-ranger-hall-of-fame.asp
6. On June 11, 2008 he received the last of his many awards by being the only Marine ever inducted into the Army Ranger Hall of Fame.

which had taken place in Cuba. Militarily speaking, it was the equivalent of getting his feet wet before the serious battles in which he would later engage. However, it did give him an idea of what war is like. The most difficult part of this mission was the forced separation from his wife Moline who was in the hospital.

Chapter 7
MOLINE BLAYLOCK

*The greatest institution in America is
the sanctity of the mother, that person
who is the center of the family.*
— **Colonel John Ripley**

John Ripley and Moline Blaylock were as unlikely a pair as
Bud and Verna had been. In the early sixties when they met,
one's social status in Radford (as in many small towns) was
indicated by the location of one's house. The farther you were
up hill from the New River, the higher your social class.
Moline, whose father was a well-respected plant manager and
founder of the local country club, lived at the top of the hill,
while the Ripleys were not only at the bottom, they were literally on the other side of the tracks. There was also a religious
difference. Moline's family was Southern Baptist, while the
Ripleys were staunchly Roman Catholic. Like most people in
town, however, the Blaylocks loved John Ripley and did not
object to his interest in their daughter.

At the time they met, Moline was an employee at Wallace's,
one of Radford's finest women's stores, and John Ripley was a
midshipman at the Naval Academy. In December 1961, he was
home for Christmas break and decided to stop in to purchase a
gift for his mother. Moline was working behind the counter.
What began with a simple purchase and a brief conversation,
rapidly turned into a serious courtship with a helpful nudge
from Bud Ripley. He knew that Moline was the right girl for
his son and took an active role as matchmaker. Once, Moline
received a forceful call from her future father-in-law. He was
going to visit his son at the Naval Academy in Annapolis and
he intended for her to go along.

"Be ready in five minutes," he told her, "you are going up

with us to see John." It was a request she could hardly refuse. Although she was seeing someone else at the time, there was something about John she liked and therefore did not put up much resistance to Bud's invitation.

PASSING UNDER A CANOPY OF SWORDS

The two saw each other sporadically over the next months, but the following spring, their courtship took on a more serious note when he invited Moline to be his guest for June Week, a series of celebrations which culminated in the students' graduation. While he was away at Basic School, she was taking instructions to become a Catholic and surprised her fiancé the following year with her intentions to convert. In May of 1964, the couple walked out of Saint Jude's Catholic Church in Radford, Virginia and passed under a canopy of Marine swords as man and wife.

From the beginning, it was clear to Moline that her husband was a serious Marine and that frequent separations were going to be a part of their lives. However, she was not one to let the grass grow under her feet. While he was away training, she acquired a position with the local school teaching first graders. The children under her care were from poor white sharecropper families. Some were so destitute, they lived in homes that were former tobacco barns with dirt floors. Seeing their unfortunate condition, Moline took it upon herself to prepare food baskets for the poorer families which she delivered during Christmas. John was more than happy to go along and help.

This scene shatters modern preconceptions of the born-with-a-silver-spoon-in-her-mouth image commonly associated with people of Moline Blaylock's social level, as well as the "tough guy" image often attributed to warriors of the caliber of John Ripley. His attitude is not surprising, considering the care he demonstrated, throughout his life, for those most in need, especially children.

FEMALE VERSION OF JOHN RIPLEY

It wasn't long before the Ripleys were expecting their first child. Everything was going fine until four months into the pregnancy. Moline started having complications and was admitted into the hospital just as her husband was about to ship out to the Dominican Republic. He stayed by her side every possible minute until the nurses announced that visiting hours were over. It was a small example of the strong union they would have during their entire lives together. Separation at that moment, so early in their marriage, was painful, but he was now a Marine and had to obey orders. Never would obedience be more difficult.

However, she was a strong lady and assured him that everything would be okay. John Ripley was not convinced and spent the rest of the night before his departure in mournful prayer for the recovery of his wife. She improved after some days and went on to give birth to a healthy baby boy who they named Stephen.

His devotion was well placed considering the supporting role she would later play within the family. Because of his many trips abroad, Moline was the backbone of the home and shouldered the majority of the responsibilities of running the house. When something needed to be done, it was always Moline who did it. She was, at one and the same time, a gracious Southern lady and the ultimate Marine Corps wife, who some described as the female version of John Ripley. There was nothing too difficult for her once she put her mind to it. Her flexibility enabled her to throw a tea party as skillfully as she could do house repairs, if the need arose. For this reason, John never failed to recognize her during awards ceremonies as the person most responsible for his achievements.

However, what stands out most in their relationship is the very motto of the Marine Corps: *Semper Fidelis*. John

Ripley's fidelity extended beyond the Corps and encom-
passed the woman he vowed to remain with for the rest of
his life. He never went out drinking with his buddies,
Stephen Ripley relates, and although he did play golf later in
life, he never understood why a person would take out four
hours on a Saturday and be away from his family to play the
game. "If they entertained they did it together," he said. "My
dad never went anywhere socially without my mom. They
were always together."

After the birth of their oldest son, they went on to have a girl
they named Mary, after the Ripley's generations-old tradition.
He often referred to her as his Princess and, since she was his
only daughter, loved her dearly. Then came Thomas who,
along with Stephen, joined the Marine Corps. Stephen
deployed with the 4th Marine Expeditionary Brigade in the first
Gulf War, while Thomas followed in his father's footsteps and
served with Force Recon. Both resigned their commissions
after having attained the rank of captain. Their youngest son,
John, graduated from VMI and, with the military downsizing
at that time, he chose to enter the business world.

Chapter 8
THE CHALLENGES OF FATHERHOOD

A leader is a man who can adapt
principles to circumstances.
—**General George Patton**

Life inside the home of John Walter Ripley was what one might expect it to be. Being a perfectionist, he placed the bar high for his children and felt that the best means for them to achieve their greatest potential was by developing their intellect. Nothing was emphasized more in the Ripley household than education.

This was due as much to the appreciation for learning he had acquired at the Naval Academy, as to the remembrance of his father's missed opportunity. Therefore, he encouraged his children to set goals. He wanted them to avoid the mistakes he made as a youth and never let them forget the time their grandfather missed the boat.

"Once you set a goal, you must never surrender," Stephen remembers his father saying. "When life becomes difficult, that's the time to buckle down, focus and work harder. Fix the goal into your mind and put every ounce of effort you have into achieving that goal. When you quit, you squander an opportunity that may never come again." Stephen remembers vividly the time his grades dipped below the standards his father thought were acceptable. He threatened his son with the task of bringing all his books home if he did not remedy the problem, such was the importance John Ripley placed on good grades.

"JUST REMEMBER THEY CAN'T KILL YOU"
While John Ripley always considered raising his children to

be his greatest achievement, they did share his youthful desire to test boundaries. This was particularly true of his son Thomas, who felt a great need to challenge the world around him. Luckily, Moline was always there to smooth things over so that her husband did not have to worry. Instead of burdening him with the problem, Moline dealt with issues head on. When one of their sons was dismissed from school, instead of picking him up, she sent him a bus ticket home, knowing that the long, lonely ride would provide the "prodigal son" a humbling perspective and time to think.

As with any family, they suffered difficulties with the children, problems that she would often have to handle by herself. However, the way Moline dealt with them showed the sensitive side of her soul. Thomas explained how she knew her husband's limitations. John Ripley was a serious Marine officer and the pressures of that position were sometimes too great to be compounded by the frustrations of household problems she was more than capable of handling. Her great sacrifice was that she became the disciplinarian of the house so that her husband could enjoy his often limited time with his children. Everyone in the household knew that Moline's bite was much harder than her husband's bark. Thus, she complimented her husband in an admirable way. In regards to Thomas, this meant a great deal of footwork.

Thomas recalls the day his father drove him to VMI where he would begin his own military career. Although he might have suffered a certain amount of trepidation at the prospect of entering a military school with such a storied tradition, he faced his fears like a man. When his father dropped him off, there was not one ounce of the sentimentality one would expect in such a father-son separation. John Ripley simply gave his son a firm handshake and a succinct bit of advice before their final farewell.

"Just remember son," he said, "they can't kill you." He then turned around, got back into the car and drove home.

PRINCIPLES OF A MARINE OFFICER

Thomas was eventually suspended as a sophomore and remembers well his father's reaction. John Ripley never got furious or stamped his feet. He simply looked at his 20-year-old son and said, "pack it up and get out. You are not to return until you are back at VMI." Moline was equally upset at her son's suspension, but her motherly heart was about to break. Thomas left the house 20 minutes later with 50 dollars in his pocket, not knowing where he would go. Moline slipped him another 20 dollars as he walked out the door. The wisdom of John Ripley would later be witnessed in the transformation which such tough love worked in the soul of his son.

"It was the best thing that could have happened to me," Thomas admits. "I took that disappointment and frustration and turned it into fuel."

He eventually ended up at a friend's house in Charlottesville, Virginia where circumstances forced him to sleep on the couch and hold down two jobs. After he was accepted at the University of Virginia (UVA), the bulk of his hard-earned money went towards his education. His only goal at that point was to demonstrate to his father and VMI that he was back in school and repentant.

Moline respected her husband's severe measures but did not allow Thomas' expulsion from the home to prevent her from visiting him often. Those visits entailed an occasional batch of her homemade chocolate chip cookies which lifted her son's spirits. When unable to visit, she sent him notes like a Thanksgiving Day card, with a simple message: "Thomas, I love you."

One day, John Ripley was invited by UVA to speak to thirty students who were contemplating a Marine career, including his son Thomas. This was the first time Thomas saw his father after being kicked out of the house. As John Ripley addressed the audience of would-be Marines, his son sat in the back of the room. Thomas remembered being mesmerized by his father's speech. It was the first time he had heard his "Principles of Being a Marine Officer." After so many years, he is still able to recall them by memory.

"The spirit of the attack. When my father would talk about this principle, he would bring up [Stonewall] Jackson's famous quote 'march to the sound of the guns.'

"Boldness, which means, as a Marine Officer, you are going to have to make decisions with limited information. Have convictions in your decisions and follow them through.

"Receptiveness for risk-taking, risk comes with the job. If you are not comfortable with risk, you need to get into a new line of work. Some people join the military nowadays to get a great college education, not realizing that we are here to do a job, to fight our country's wars, and that involves risk. We cannot make this a risk-free proposition.

"Endurance, what he called the rule of the marathon runner. The body will always go further than the mind. The reason why people fail to finish marathons is not because they can't do it. It has to do with conditioning the mind. The mind is the strongest muscle in the body. Condition that muscle and you will be able to exceed all your expectations.

"Be decisive. This means acting, even when you don't have all the information. Being bold and being decisive are two different things. Being decisive means being a leader.

"Sense of mission, sense of duty, mission first, Marines always. It's a catch phrase which others use, but one which John Ripley literally invented. When he told anyone about the Marines it was always, 'mission first, Marines always. If you don't do your job, then we are going to have to send someone else here and they are probably going to lose people doing it.'"

Thomas went on to describe how these principles hit him like a bullet. He could not figure out why he had not heard them before.

"I had known the man for twenty years," he concluded, "but it was like a different person up there talking to me." The expulsion from the house and that speech turned out to be the turning points in his life.

At the end of his talk, John Ripley gave his son, and the other thirty prospective Marines, a card with those principles written on it. He carried that card in his pocket, next to the picture of his wife, every day of his Marine career.

It was because of John Ripley's tough love and his son's own hard work and determination that Thomas was accepted into Officer Candidate School (OCS) in Quantico, Virginia. He graduated top in his class at OCS with the distinction of Honor Man. As a result of his performance, Thomas was readmitted to VMI as the number one Marine officer candidate in the nation, with a full two-year scholarship.

"We made plenty of mistakes," he reminisced, "and if it were not for the bond of family, none of us would have seen 18. Our father gave us everything. He never had an expensive car, took individual vacations or had lavish things. All of that went to our education and betterment. He was a selfless parent."

RIPLEY VACATIONS

Some of the most amusing stories of John Ripley, the father, concerned family outings which resembled Marine training more than a vacation.

"In our house it was 100% all the time and this held true for vacations," Thomas said. "We would drive half the night to the beach. After arriving at 2 a.m., we did what every normal family would do—we went for a swim."

On another occasion, the family took a day trip to Martha's Vineyard. John Ripley rented five bicycles and they peddled around the entire island. Thomas was only ten at the time, but remembers all too well how they found out firsthand that it is twenty-seven miles around Martha's Vineyard. Similarly, while visiting Yosemite in the early spring one year, all the boys had to swim across the Merced River.

The most humorous story he recalled was when the Ripley family took part in a church ski trip to Blue Knob in Claysburg, Pennsylvania. By the time the bus pulled to the top of the mountain, everyone was standing in the aisle excitedly anticipating an enjoyable day of skiing. When the doors opened, they were hit in the face with a freezing cold gust of 40mph winds. It felt like the North Pole. The would-be-vacationers from Virginia simply stared out the door with a look of terror, as John Ripley joyfully led his family into the rigors of the Allegheny Mountains. They were the only ones who got off the bus and the only family on the mountain that day. Thomas remembers sitting on a ski lift with his dad after their first run down the mountain.

"Aren't you glad we are out here?" a smiling John Ripley said, as gale force winds tossed their chair from side to side.

SKILLS OF A CIVIL WAR SURGEON

"Everything he did was done to an extreme," said his son Stephen. When the family went camping, for example, it meant doing so at the base of a mountain and living off the land. After planning one such trip in Oregon, Stephen described their arrival at the national park:

"[Our] family drove past the other campers," he said. "Then past the serious hikers and then the mountain men, until we finally stopped at some isolated spot where we set up base camp as if we were going to climb a mountain."

If there were a medical problem during their time out, it was no problem for John Ripley. His children used to tease him that he was like a Civil War surgeon because no matter what you had, from a splinter to a broken thumb, he would have a remedy.

"He would take your hand, bend your arm back and sit on it, so that you could not get away," Stephen explained. "Then with a popsicle stick, tweezers and pins, or whatever was available, he would perform the necessary 'surgery.'" Thomas specifically recalls his father's dental skills. One day, he was complaining about having to wear braces and demanded they be removed. He was obviously thinking about a doctor doing the work and was surprised when his father approached him with a pair of pliers and a look of determination. The braces were removed and it is unlikely that Thomas ever complained about such things again.

Chapter 9
A CATHOLIC MARINE

*If you can be a good Catholic you
can be a good Marine.*[1]
— **Colonel John Ripley**

Perhaps the most valuable lesson John Ripley would instill
in his children was the importance of practicing the Faith. The
way he practiced religion was refreshingly manly, without the
sentimentality often seen in those who like to appear pious.
This entailed a militantly regular attendance at Sunday Mass
which was for him an important aspect of life in the Ripley
home. He was zealous that everyone fulfill their Sunday obligation. If his children ever complained, he immediately
reminded them of the difficulty he had in practicing the Faith
as a boy. The story he frequently told was about how he and his
brothers cleaned up the beer-soaked floors in Radford's
American Legion Hall so that Catholics could go to Mass.

If, by chance, one of them arrived late, the entire family
would attend that Mass and the next one also. It goes without
saying that the children were never late, nor did they even
think about leaving right after Communion, a lamentable custom among so many Catholics today. John Ripley would take
his post at the end of the pew and stand as a silent sentinel until
Mass was over. The Ripley children knew that they were going
to be there from start to finish, along with anyone else who
happened to be sitting with them.

"KNEEL OR SIT, DON'T DO BOTH"
They were also expected to kneel straight. John Ripley took

---

1. Mel Oberg, "Colonel Takes Command at College," *Richmond Times Dispatch*,
July 17, 1992.

a great pride in being a Marine and always maintained an impeccable posture, especially during Mass. He detested the relaxed kneeling position of so many able-bodied Catholics and trained his children not to follow their poor example.

"When you use the kneeler, do not rest your bottom on the pew," Thomas Ripley quoted his father as saying, "kneel or sit, but don't do both." All that was needed to correct one of his sons who adopted the irreverent position was a stern glance and snap of his fingers. If the Church were full and no kneelers were available, Stephen recalls his father kneeling on the floor. Nevertheless, his way of practicing religion was anything but ostentatious. At the end of his life, he attended Mass on a daily basis, but never called attention to himself. When Stephen was sent overseas during the First Gulf War, he looked for every opportunity to attend Mass because of his father's example.

"Not because I was afraid," he said, "but because I needed it. It was a part of my life growing up... due to the influence of my parents."

Stephen also remembers how religion played a unique role in his father's life. Although it was rare, they did notice how he would sometimes go days without eating. It only dawned on them later that he was fasting. Stephen was quick to point out that their father was no saint and speculated the reason for this penitential practice might have been, "his way to focus and gain perspective." However, he did these pious exercises without calling attention to himself and when asked the reason for his actions, he simply declined comment.

AN EXAMPLE FOR OTHER MARINES

It is curious to note how John Ripley's Faith also impacted those who served under him, like Don Shomette of Radford, Virginia. He is a convert and, while he was being catechized, noticed the similarities between the Marine Corps and the Catholic Church. When he saw Catholicism as a religion that is "bold, radical, uncompromising and gung ho," the first person he thought of was John Ripley. He saw him as a man who was both a good Marine and practicing Catholic, without jeopardizing his Faith or ability to lead men in battle.

"When I think of Catholicism, I think of John Ripley," he said, "those two are one and the same. He embodied the Faith. It wasn't something he put on just for Sundays. It was something that probably came natural to him."

This was apparent in his way of speaking. As a rule, he never used foul language. When producers approached him about making a movie on his life, he agreed as long as two conditions were respected. First of all, he did not want the person portraying him using foul language because, he said, "I don't use such words." The closest thing to a curse word the Commandant of the Marine Corps, General James Conway, ever heard him use was "doggonit."[2]

Secondly, he would not tolerate his character having an extramarital relationship. He knew the artistic license often taken by Hollywood and its ability to gratuitously portray positive role models committing adultery. There is nothing more harmful to admiration than seeing one's heroes portrayed in such ways. John Ripley would have none of this.

"I have never been, nor will I ever be, unfaithful to my wife," he told them. A man like John Ripley would never think of dishonoring himself or his spouse in a way that has become so common for many men in our society. With such a chivalrous and loyal attitude towards Moline, it is no surprise that he referred to her, on occasion, as his "Queen."

---

2. Comment General Conway made during Colonel Ripley's funeral eulogy.

* * *

Stephen was barely a year old in the summer of 1966 when John Ripley received his orders to go to Vietnam. His time in the Dominican Republic was merely an appetizer to the extreme situations he would face in the war zone of Southeast Asia.

Before leaving, he took advantage to visit with family members and help his brother Michael move into a new apartment. The hard work did not bother him and since it was his last summer home, he was enjoying Michael's company. Late in the day they stopped for a break and were enjoying cold drinks and sandwiches on the back porch, when they noticed a disturbing scene unfold before their eyes.

Behind the apartment building was a large field surrounded by a chain link fence. A three-year-old boy, left unattended, had wandered into the field. Moments later a ferocious German shepherd appeared on the scene and began barking in the child's face. The hysterical toddler attracted the attention of those in the area, who knew he was moments away from being mauled. Everyone was frozen in a state of shock except for John Ripley and his brother. They jumped off the porch, hurdled the fence, ran thirty yards through the wet field and attacked the dog. After saving the child from certain danger and possible death, they calmly returned to the porch and finished their sandwiches. The fearlessness that John Ripley showed on this occasion was about to be repeated in defense of the Vietnamese people oppressed by a tyrannical Communist regime.

Moline said goodbye to her husband in September. He was on his way to Camp Pendleton, California where he would prepare other Marines for the rigors of war in Southeast Asia. She did not realize that the next time she would see him would be on the evening news.

Chapter 10
A WISE AND FEARLESS WARRIOR

*"Never take counsel from your fears. Your
enemy is more worried than you are.
Numerical superiority, while useful, is not
vital to offensive action. The fact that you
are attacking induces the enemy to believe
you are stronger than he is."*
— **General Stonewall Jackson**

David Counts of Chilhowie, Virginia was a nineteen-year-old private when he arrived at Camp Pendleton. John Ripley was a twenty-six-year-old captain. Although senior officers always intimidated him, David quickly found out that there was nothing to fear in the man assigned to train him for war.

What impressed him most about John Ripley was his wisdom. The story that stuck out in his mind occurred one hot day when a private ran out of water. Seeing this, another Marine attempted to sell him his. When Captain Ripley heard about this, he became furious. Without losing his temper or using profanity, he called everyone together and told them to pour their water on the ground. One can only imagine the reaction of the tired and thirsty Marines.

"When one person is out of water," he told the stunned audience, "everyone is out of water." John Ripley could not conceive an individual profiting from others in the unit who were in need. The example he gave his men in training and war was to think about the needs of others first before satisfying their own.

"It was the way a perfect Marine officer would act," said Mr. Counts. "I said right then, 'he has the wisdom of Solomon.'"

* * *

After arriving in Vietnam in October of 1966, John Ripley

was quickly put in command of Lima Rifle Company, 3rd Battalion, 3rd Marine Regiment. Since Vietnam was a small unit war, the rifle company was ideal. It was mobile and efficient. It was also one of the most coveted positions in the Marine Corps.

By the time he arrived in Southeast Asia, then 2nd Lieutenant, now Captain, Eddie McCourt had been fighting the North Vietnamese Army (NVA) for thirteen months and was in charge of India Company 1st Platoon. Although he was quite different from Captain Ripley in many ways, they did have some similarities. Both men were made for war and both liked to be in the heat of the fight.

Captain McCourt had already acquired a legendary status for his courage and a good indicator of his effectiveness as a combat leader was the song written about him by Lance Corporal Michael Baronowski. Michael was a seasoned veteran with only two months to go on his tour when he composed the "Ballad of Fort McCourt" in honor of his fearless commander. The next day he was killed while walking the point for the commander who had earned his respect. As legendary as Eddie McCourt was, he held a similar veneration for John Ripley.

"He was fearless," said Captain McCourt, "and I always felt comfortable when he was around. 'Rip' was an NVA/VC magnet. My Marines and I used to request to be assigned to one of Lima Company's flanks because we were sure to see a lot of action."[1]

"INTO THE GATES OF HELL"

That action came in a big way during a foot patrol on the afternoon of November 28, 1966, when Captain McCourt's men were given a break and put in reserve, not realizing the danger that lay ahead. As the first platoons of India Company passed through a group of hedgerows, they overlooked three

---

1. Richard Botkin, unpublished portion.

NVA regulars hiding in the bush. When McCourt's reserve platoon passed through the same area, the NVA took off running. His Marines, anxious for combat, pursued them without realizing they were running headlong into an ambush. McCourt's men became confused and didn't know where to fire while the rest of the company remained pinned down in the open. As McCourt began marking the enemy's location with tracers, he noticed that Lima Company, now 75 yards to his right, was firing into the same location. He breathed a sigh of relief to see John Ripley in the area with a company that had earned a reputation for being "ambush busters."

"I knew right then that victory was ours," said McCourt. "My men and I would follow [Captain Ripley] into the gates of hell because we all knew he would lead us back out."

Like most men who experience combat, Captain McCourt knew the secret to surviving in the heat of battle. While playing football for the Marine Corps, he noticed that those who played the hardest were injured the least. The same thing, he reasoned, applied to war. Those who fought the hardest lived the longest. Such was the case with John Ripley.

His ability to fight against overwhelming odds was as much a result of his mental strength as his physical abilities. When he was in a firefight, he didn't listen to his body, but kept his mind focused on the mission. It didn't matter if he were tired, hungry or even wounded. He did not stop, give in or quit until the mission was accomplished. It was mission first, his personal needs last.

AGGRESSIVE LEADERSHIP

His consistent victories were also due to his aggressive style of leadership. In his mind, success in battle comes from being on the offense, whereas excessive caution is inherently defeatist. His three great principles of war, after his hero Stonewall

Jackson, were: attack, attack and attack![2] More important than being a fighter was the example he set for his men.

"Your unit has to see you as a leader," he would say, "and they have to gain confidence in your confidence."[3] This meant being a role model for others to follow. In this way, he became a motivating factor for those around him and if they thought about quitting, even for one minute, all they needed to do was look at him to find inspiration to fight on.

His style of leadership, as pointed out by David Counts, was also eminently wise. He knew the principles of war which had been handed down for generations and followed them to a T even when others chose not to. As a rule, when they were on foot patrols, he always had his men dig a foxhole at the end of the day. An hour after sunset, he would move some distance away and have them dig another one. This drove his men crazy until, one day, the enemy bombed the first foxhole they had dug. Had they not made a second one, all of them would have been killed. His men never complained after that.

Along with wisdom, he also possessed a fearlessness which began to earn him a reputation. This was illustrated by another story Captain McCourt told about a firefight that became particularly ugly. In the middle of the battle, he noticed someone dangerously exposing himself to heavy enemy fire. Not realizing who it was, he screamed out to his radioman, "tell that Marine to take cover."

"That ain't no Marine," the radioman replied, "that's Captain Ripley."[4] Despite his short time in Vietnam, he was making his mark as a leader that possessed a high degree of determination.

2. Cf. Major Ted McKeldin, USMCR, *From the Horse's Mouth: Selected Thoughts on Small Unit Leadership* (Quantico, Virginia: Marine Corps Association, 1999), p. 19.
3. Otto Lehrack, *No Shining Armor: The Marines at War in Vietnam: An Oral History* (Lawrence: University Press of Kansas, 1992), p. 3.
4. Richard Botkin, unpublished portion.

Chapter 11
A LEGEND IS BORN

To drop dead is honorable in the
pursuit of duty, whereas to quit is
the highest form of dishonor.
— **Colonel John Ripley**

Captain Ripley's tenacity was nowhere more apparent than during a battle that occurred on March 2, 1967. It was a day he earned legendary status. The conflict began at 7:00 a.m. when Lima Company was assaulted by a sniper who they quickly dispatched. Moments later, one of his men captured a sentry with a sophisticated radio, equipped with a knee key. The radio's complexity was a bad omen of things to come.

After investigating the scene further, Captain Ripley realized that they had stumbled into an extensive base camp of a battalion level unit. Their arrival caused the NVA to flee. Moments later, when all hell broke loose, they found out the enemy had not traveled far. They were hit with everything from automatic weapons and small arms to grenades and mortars. When Captain Ripley gave the order to fix bayonets, the men of Lima Company knew that their situation was serious.

Corporal Jerry Larsen was fighting alongside Captain Ripley. After being shot in both legs, Larsen refused to lie down and, in an act of defiance, forced himself into a sitting position. He then stuck spent cartridges into the holes in his legs to prevent further loss of blood which enabled him to fight on.[1] Through it all, Captain Ripley remained calm in spite of the death and carnage that surrounded him.

One scene Ripley witnessed was that of a fellow Marine lying in a foxhole next to his dead friend whose face had been

---

1. Cf. TFP lectures.

blown off.[2] The shell-shocked Marine kept fighting the enemy, but the signs of stress were evident when he was seen patting his dead comrade on the shoulder, reassuring him that help was on the way.

RIPLEY'S RAIDERS

As the casualties mounted, a helicopter arrived on the scene with veteran Brigadier General Michael Patrick Ryan aboard. He had earned the Navy Cross during the battle of Tarawa in World War II and was showing equal courage by attempting to drop medical supplies for the wounded.

With the amount of fire they were receiving, Captain Ripley waved them off, knowing that it was foolhardy to attempt a medical drop. Crew members on board the helicopter frantically kicked the much-needed packages of medical supplies out the door. As the aircraft began to pull away, a mortar hit one of the boxes and exploded. Shrapnel tore through the air and several people, including Captain Ripley, were injured. The impact threw him and his radio operator airborne.

"I'll never forget the sensation of being blown through the air and looking over at my operator [who] was 180 degrees inverted," he said. "His feet were straight up. His head was straight down. He still had his head set in his ear."[3]

Captain Ripley came down hard on the muzzle of his gun and broke some ribs. In spite of his injuries, he refused to leave his men and fought on.

"Things became progressively worse," he said later, "but we fought on, harder and harder, knowing we would prevail at the end of the day although it wasn't immediately apparent how."[4]

With such a display of courage and leadership, TV crews

---

2. Otto Lehrack, p. 127.
3. Ibid., p. 125.
4. TFP Lectures.

and cameramen arrived on the scene, anxious to capture some of the action. Moline saw news of her husband on television back in Blacksburg, Virginia and it wasn't long before the coverage of his exploits made it to the print media. Two weeks after the March 2 battle, a member of Lima Company received a news clipping from home telling about the deeds of a group of Marines they appropriately dubbed "Ripley's Raiders."[5] The men of Lima Company latched onto the name and a legend was born.

"HE WAS FEARLESS"

Because of the superior leadership qualities of their heroic captain, "Ripley's Raiders" were able to drive back the much superior force that attacked them that day, but it came at a great cost to their unit. They had entered the fight with over two hundred men, including attachments. At the end of the day, only fifteen remained standing. The rest had either been killed or wounded. Intense battle was a common thing during his first tour in Vietnam. Hardly a day went by without some action.

"People find it hard to believe that I never slept in Vietnam," Ripley said. "Never was I fully unconscious. Anytime the handset on the radio clicked, I was fully awake immediately."[6] The amount of tension he experienced, always trying to do the right thing and hoping everything would turn out okay for his men, was enormous. A member of the dental contact team noticed this while examining Captain Ripley's teeth the day after a particularly grueling battle. Everything in his mouth was bleeding and the dentist determined it was most likely caused by stress.[7]

Through it all, John Ripley remained steadfast and during

---

5. Rich Botkin, *Ride the Thunder: A Vietnam War Story of Honor and Triumph* (Santa Monica: WND Books, 2009) p. 95.
6. Major Ted McKeldin USMCR, p. 5.
7. Cf. Otto Lehrack, p. 167.

the countless skirmishes his men encountered, they unani-
mously attested to his courage under fire. Don Wolfe of
Western Pennsylvania fought with "Ripley's Raiders" and
witnessed him do things, on several occasions, that were
worthy of the Medal of Honor. Although the pain of remembering wartime events has left his overall picture of what
occurred cloudy, the details of one incident remained crystal
clear in his mind.

It was a day when "Ripley's Raiders" were being over-
whelmed by a lone machine gunner concealed inside the safety of his nest. As the automatic weapon filled the air with hot
lead, a frightened Wolfe vividly remembered John Ripley
charging across the field directly into the line of fire. Moments
later, he singlehandedly silenced the machine gunner saving
his men from further harm.

"He was just fearless," said Wolfe. Those who fought under
him in Lima Company affirmed that his "resoluteness and old-
fashioned bravery sustained them all" and they "credited their
survival in Vietnam specifically to him having led them."[8]

A RISK TAKER

One of those men is John Solbach. He was a green 19-year-
old private from Clays Center, Kansas when he arrived at
Vietnam. He is proud to have spent his entire tour with
"Ripley's Raiders." He met John Ripley on his first day in the
country in a place called Lima Hill. This patch of ground had
many other names. Some called it "mud hill," perhaps because
it was located just south of Mudder's Ridge. It could also have
been due to the fact they were usually ankle deep in sludge.
John Ripley just called it the "punch bowl." Very early in his

8.   Richard Botkin, "Honor the Warrior: "Ripley's Raiders" 40-Year Reunion," originally published on World Net Daily on March 27, 2007, currently available at:
http://hughhewitt.townhall.com/blog/g/24e2518b-2104-40c0-9c02-ce3a12fb7a34.

tour, Solbach heard amazing stories about his new commander's capacity to take control of a crisis situation.

"He took risks that other people couldn't take," he said, "but they were calculated risks. When you are really talented, you can do that. When the bullets started flying, that's when his 'machinery' started to work and his 'sprockets' started to turn. That's when the 'mechanism' came to life."

According to Mr. Solbach, John Ripley got medals for things that would have gotten other, less competent men court-martialed. Rather than call him a risk taker, Mr. Solbach defined him more precisely as a risk manager, but quickly added that, "if you are going to be a risk manager, you have to go where the risk is.

"He knew that regardless of what he got into, he could figure a way to get out of it, to turn it to his favor and he always did. He was well trained, he was in good shape, his mind was sharp, he understood his company and what they could do."

Chapter 12
UNIQUE SIDE OF A WARRIOR

There is not a person in war who is not
scared, but you can't let fear control you.
— **Colonel John Ripley**

When one considers the brutality of war as seen by John Ripley, he is amazed at how the Marine captain was able to maintain elevation of spirit in such extreme conditions. Pacifists and hippies of the time were quick to characterize our men who fought in the jungles of Vietnam as insensitive "baby killers." This was not the case, especially in regards to John Ripley. He was a model battlefield commander who took care of his men. All of this was due to an essential principle of leadership which he memorized. The basic ingredient a true leader must possess, he once said, is character, which he defined as:

> All those elements that require a person to focus on others rather than himself; to postpone one's own personal desires—what I want—until the needs of others have been looked after and satisfied.[1]

SENSITIVITY TOWARDS THE VIETNAMESE PEOPLE
For John Ripley, this focus on others included the Vietnamese people. Nineteen-year-old private John Solbach described an episode that occurred one evening in 1967 when members of "Ripley's Raiders" were returning from a field operation. It was already past dark and they were alarmed upon their arrival by the sound of some noisy pigs rooting around in a trash dump just outside the perimeter. This represented a security threat because it interfered with their ability to hear enemy activity and gave away their position at the same time.

---

1. TFP lectures.

The men knew something had to be done and took measures to remedy the problem. The solution for them seemed simple. Kill the pigs! Before doing so, they sought their commander's approval and much to their surprise, he refused.

"That livestock might belong to a farmer who needs it to sustain his family," John Solbach quoted him saying. The pigs were saved and the men of Lima Company were told to find an alternative.

"I remember at first feeling shame for not thinking of that myself," said Solbach, "and then admiration for the decency of our skipper. That decency was an essential part of him. It was a filter through which he ran everything else, something for which he was not feared, but loved. It influenced the attitude and the demeanor of his officers and men, even when we were called upon to be the wolves we were trained to be."

Captain Stephen Moore also fought with John Ripley and remembered a humorous story that illustrated the more painful side of his sensitivity towards the Vietnamese people and their customs. It occurred one day when they were sitting down to have a wonderful steak dinner. This was a luxury in the field.

"As these huge juicy steaks were being taken off the grill," he said, "and Rip was about to devour them, a Vietnamese soldier approached. He had prepared a special meal for the senior officer, who happened to be Captain Ripley." He could have respectfully refused, but realized that this gesture was an important part of the Vietnamese culture. To them it was an honor to serve the commanding officer and to refuse would have been an insult.

"I can still see his face," said Captain Moore, "as our people took his steak away and the Vietnamese replaced it with a specially prepared fish plate. His look was like that of a kid whose candy had been taken away. He watched it all the way as they took it away, but graciously accepted the meal provided by his host."

FATHERLY CARE FOR HIS MEN

This is pretty much how Ron Darden remembered his former captain. He recalls very clearly the day he joined "Ripley's Raiders" as a 19-year-old lance corporal. He had been wounded in battle and the first day back, he was put on guard duty. No sooner had he assumed his post than he noticed a solitary figure approach out of the darkness. He commanded the individual to identify himself. One can only imagine his surprise when the mystery man jumped into the foxhole next to him. It was Captain Ripley.

Darden was shocked by the visit, but even more so by the series of questions that followed. The solicitous captain asked him where he was from, if he was married and how his parents were getting along without him. The atmosphere of the unexpected nightly chat must have resembled more the visit of a chaplain than that of a battlefield commander for the calming effect it had over him. Early in the conversation, Darden was honest about the fear he had upon his arrival in Vietnam. Captain Ripley reassured him with a Patton-like response.

"There is not a person in war who is not scared," he told him, "but you can't let fear control you." By the time their talk was over, Darden was a changed man.

What impressed him most about his commander was that he never asked one of his men to do what he was incapable of doing himself. He was truly a leader who led from the front, rather than pushed from the rear.

"If he wanted you to go up a hill, he would grab you and take you, himself," said Darden. "But he was right there with you all the way and it didn't matter what he was facing: small arms, full contact, mortars, artillery. He was crawling around directing your fire. He never backed down from a fight and was always leading and encouraging us from the very front of the battle."

Darden, who went on to earn a Silver Star when he ran into the middle of a firefight to save a wounded Marine's life, described another side of John Ripley.

"I saw him openly weep when he found the body of a tortured Marine… who should have rotated out a day before, but instead went with Rip to help another company that had been ambushed."[2] He was capable of showing such emotion because he cared for his men like a father. They saw the tender side, but also the disciplinarian.

"SHAVING MARKED THE DAY"

On one occasion, they were in the punch bowl, a place John Ripley described as "terribly unlovely," with "mud up to their knees."[3] He knew the effect that such conditions had on his men and took it upon himself to provide elements of civilization one would not expect to find in such circumstances. The cook, who normally stays in the rear, was ordered to the front lines and told to make hot coffee for the men returning from patrol. He was frightened to death by the bullets flying all around and probably complained about such orders, but the effect hot coffee had on the rest of Lima Company was enormous.

The cook also provided another luxury in the field: hot water for shaving. John Ripley expected the men under his leadership to look and act like Marines. This meant being well-shaven every day because, in the extreme conditions of war, he noticed that men can easily become desensitized to those details that maintain discipline and personal dignity in the

---

2. Ron Darden, "Marine's Marine and a Hero Lost," Letter to the editor, *Bradenton Herald*, November 11, 2008.
3. Otto Lehrack, p. 113.

Marine Corps. "Shaving marked the day and it also marked us," he said. "It was a clean start to the day."[4]

This care for his men is what drove John Ripley, on another occasion, to become angry when he noticed that the trousers of one of his troops were getting so worn out, that the seat of his pants was nearly gone. He felt this was inexcusable considering they were fighting for the richest nation on earth. However, he didn't resign himself to idle anger, but personally solved the problem by acquiring some new pants for the Marine.

This fact is known because of a letter he received from the grateful mother who appreciated his concern for the wellbeing of her son. Although it is hard to understand how, John Ripley kept up a lively correspondence with his men's family members back home. He often sent letters of praise for courageous actions. At other times, he wrote painful missives recognizing the valor of those that didn't make it, like Lieutenant Terry Heekin who was killed in the March 2 battle described above. Some excerpts from the correspondence between Lieutenant Heekin's parents and John Ripley are worth reproducing here.

> Dear Captain Ripley,
>   We wish to take this means to thank you for the letter concerning the death of our son, 2nd Lieutenant Terry Heekin. In it you said that you are better men [sic] because of Terry and we feel Terry was a better man because of you...Terry died because he believed so strongly in what he was doing... We are thankful and grateful to you and your men for the sacrifice you are making for our freedom. May God walk with you.
>   Sincerely,
>   *Mr. and Mrs. Elroy Lloyd*

---

4. Major Ted McKeldin, USMCR, p. 8.

John Ripley's reaction was profound and, considering the horrific conditions under which he was fighting, the gentility of his response is noteworthy.

> To Mrs. Lloyd,
> Many of us from time to time have selfish feelings of sacrifice that possibly result from being away from home and family. It's easy for us to feel sorry for ourselves, particularly as we are here missing the things we enjoy the most. For this, I must offer an apology. I will admit to sharing these feelings from time to time, but after reading your card I shall never be able to again.
> ...The message which you deliver, perhaps unknowingly, is that our daily problems and occasional sacrifices, which may seem bad, may never compare with the ultimate one which you and others at home have suffered...
> I pray that my service here may in some way serve to perpetuate the spirit that you represent. Thank God I have the privilege to serve.
>   *John Ripley*[5]

FROM *TRIPLE THREAT* TO MORTAL DANGER

During his first tour in Vietnam, Captain Ripley was injured on four separate occasions and finally forced to evacuate. After recovering from his wounds, he quickly returned to the front lines to finish his tour. He came home with a Silver Star, Bronze Star with V for valor and Purple Heart. He would have received several more of the latter, but refused to report all his injuries. He knew that commanders who attracted as much

---

5. This excerpt is from a draft of the letter Colonel Ripley actually sent. The author found this draft in Colonel Ripley's personal file cabinet.

attention as he, would be pulled off the front lines and feared this would jeopardize his chance to fight.

After his first tour of duty in Vietnam, he studied at the Amphibious Warfare School in Quantico, Virginia before being assigned as Infantry Captain's Monitor at the Marine Corps Headquarters in Washington, D.C.

His constant search for perfection distinguished him among warriors. This must have been what drove him to the northern regions of Norway in the winter of 1969 to train with the British Royal Commandos. During his time there, he served with the 3rd Commando Brigade in Singapore, the Gurkha Rifles and 40th Commando on a post-and-station tour that included combat.

He also had the unique distinction of being the first "Yankee" to command a British unit when he was put in charge of "Y" Company 45 Commando, Royal Marines. He served with them for two consecutive winters 150 miles above the Arctic Circle, where winds reached in excess of 40 mph and temperatures sometimes plummeted to 40 degrees below zero. During that time, he completed the Royal Marine Mountain and Arctic Warfare courses. This was no small thing, considering that, "only the elite members of Her Majesty's forces are permitted to take such training or are capable of meeting its fantastic demands on both body and spirit."[6]

One of the many things he learned while with the Royal Marines was a lesson which would be useful in the next chapter of his life. It had to do with physical fitness. "Americans," he said, "have a fixation with upper body strength which has more to do with appearance than actual strength."[7] During his time with the British Special Forces, he learned the value of

---

6. Mels Jeffries, "Radford Man finds Beauty and Danger in Arctic Land," *Radford News Journal*, March 18, 1970.
7. TFP Lectures

endurance which he defined as the "mental attitude that your mind imposes over your physical limitations." An attitude, he said, "that you will never admit defeat for any reason."[8]

Besides this valuable lesson, he received a distinction among members of Force Recon. He had already endured three of the toughest military programs in the world, by completing the British Commando Course he was now considered a *quad body*, a title shared by only two other men on the planet at that time. He was no longer simply a *triple threat*, but a mortal danger to anyone in his path. This would become painfully clear to the North Vietnamese all too soon, as John Ripley would return to Vietnam and accomplish a feat so stunning that it would echo throughout the world.

---

8. Major Ted McKeldin, USMCR, p. 18.

Chapter 13
THE LAST ADVISORS

Do not take counsel of your fears.
— General George Patton

Dong Ha, a tiny village located just below the Demilitarized Zone (DMZ), was the central stage for the deciding moment of Colonel Ripley's life.

To appreciate the story, it is helpful to recall the involvement of the Marines in the war effort, especially that of Lieutenant Colonel Victor Croizat. When John Ripley was still a teenager in 1954, Croizat was picking up the pieces of a broken Vietnam following the French defeat in the battle of Dien Bien Phu. After the partitioning of Vietnam and the implementation of Communism in the North, over 800,000 Vietnamese refugees, who did not want to live under the despotic regime, made their way south and were assisted by Croizat. His "untiring effort at first to rescue, and then to resettle the war-ravaged refugees had made him nearly a national hero in South Vietnam."[1]

Lieutenant Colonel Croizat would also go on to establish a South Vietnamese Marine Corps (SVMC) which would, under the direction of American advisors, develop into a serious fighting force. The relationship between the newly established SVMC and the Americans was cemented by a bond of trust. There was no hardship that the Vietnamese Marines suffered which was not also endured by their American counterparts.

"Basic to the creed was the sharing of food, danger, hardship and discomfort in the field. Wherever the Vietnamese commander hung his hammock, his American advisor hung his nearby."[2]

---

1. Colonel Gerald Turley, *The Easter Offensive: The Last American Advisors, Vietnam 1972* (Annapolis, Md.: US Naval Institute Press, 1995) p. 7.
2. Donald Price, *First Marine Captured in Vietnam* (Jefferson, NC: McFarland, 2007) p. 10.

Lieutenant Colonel Croizat would go on to earn the respected title of Co-Van, Vietnamese for "trusted friend." Out of the
6,000 American advisors in the 20 years following the formation of the Vietnamese Marines, only 600 would earn this title.
Captain John Ripley was one of the last.

During his previous tour of duty, there had been well
over 500,000 American troops in Vietnam. In the later part of
1971, only 27,000 remained due to President Nixon's
"Vietnamization" program which turned the war over to the
Vietnamese. One of those men was Lieutenant Colonel (now
Colonel) Gerald Turley. He arrived in 1972 and his flight to
Vietnam was anything but encouraging. While he was waiting
in the Okinawa airport for his departure to Saigon, American
soldiers returning to the U.S. taunted him. "You will be sorry!"
He would soon find out more fully what they meant.

Upon his arrival, he was integrated into the country in record
time and assigned as the Assistant Senior Marine Advisor. One
of the first things he received from his commanding officer was
the Senior Advisor's journal. It was the equivalent of a ship captain's log with meticulous notes concerning the formation and
growth of the Vietnamese Marine Corps since the time of
Croizat. As Lieutenant Colonel Turley paged through the journal, he was told that he, like John Ripley, would be one of the
last advisors in Vietnam. What he did not know was the intensity of his involvement and the strange set of circumstances that
would ultimately unite him and Ripley.

The Easter Offensive and the destruction of the Dong Ha
Bridge were the defining points of both men's lives. The
offensive occurred in March of 1972 when the North
Vietnamese launched a massive invasion of South Vietnam.
Lieutenant Colonel Turley was the man who, against the
direct orders of higher command, gave the order for John
Ripley to blow the bridge.

Colonel Turley submitted a detailed report of the events of April 2. Because of his proximity to the situation and his direct command of operations at the time, his record of what happened is most interesting.

Chapter 14
THE RING OF STEEL

*My attitude had always been, no obstacle is too
great [or] too numerous... there is simply no
place for negativism in the life of a Marine.*
— Colonel John Ripley

The circumstances which led up to the destruction of the
bridge began on the evening of March 29, 1972. Lieutenant
Colonel Turley had taken a trip to Phu Bi to meet with all the
Marine advisors assigned to Vietnamese Marine Corps
brigades in the vicinity of Quang Tri and Dong Ha. After
spending the night there, he traveled to the 3rd Army of the
Republic of Vietnam (ARVN) Division Headquarters at the Ai
Tu combat base located just south of Dong Ha.

Upon his arrival, he met with the 3rd ARVN Division staff
and the commanding officer of the U.S. Army Advisory Team
155 for a series of briefings followed by lunch with Majors
James Joy and Jim Smock. It turned out to be a fortuitous
meeting with Smock, considering the supporting role he would
play in the days that followed.

No sooner had they walked out the front door of the mess
hall, when the area was suddenly struck by intense artillery
fire. In the subsequent days, the bombardment continued
unabated with over 1,500 rounds a day raining down on the
beleaguered South Vietnamese forces. Marines and soldiers in
the Command and Control (COC) bunker were running on
pure adrenaline since the intensity of battle gave little time for
eating and sleeping.

On the morning of March 31, Lieutenant Colonel Turley
was ordered to fill in for the G3 Operations Advisor of the U.S.
Army Advisory team who requested to be medically evacuated because of combat fatigue. This was an extraordinary turn

of events because he was a lieutenant colonel in the Marines surrounded by senior Army officers who, besides outranking him, were more knowledgeable of the overall battlefield scenario. He reluctantly accepted the position of Senior Advisor, but only after obtaining the name and social security number of the officer thrusting this burden upon his shoulders as evidence of his emergency orders. He would remain in that volatile and chaotic situation for the next four days. During that time, as many as nine U.S. Army colonels passed through the COC bunker and reviewed the desperate situation, yet refused to relieve him of his advisor responsibilities.

LEATHERNECK SQUARE
    Circumstances could not have provided a better man to deal with the extreme conditions than Gerald Turley, a tough Irish Catholic, who never backed down from a fight. Over the next days, he would face the fight of his life. His newly acquired area of responsibility was the five northernmost provinces of South Vietnam called I CORPS. The buffer zone between his COC bunker and the DMZ was a patch of real estate appropriately named "Leatherneck Square," referring to the age-old nickname for Marines. It consisted in a series of firebases manned by South Vietnamese Marines and American advisors. Key among them was Camp Carroll with its 1,500 troops and twenty-six artillery pieces. Its guns were essential in providing support and protection for the coveted Dong Ha Bridge located on Highway 1. This thoroughfare was the main North/South freeway linking the Communist north with the fledgling South Vietnam.
    The brunt of the assault, beginning on March 30, was directed at the northern arc of Leatherneck Square, an area just south of the DMZ known as the "Ring of Steel." This included four infantry divisions supported by Surface to Air

A youthful Pauline Ripley. John Ripley's grandmother was described as "culture and refinement personified."

John Ripley (left) with his grandmother Pauline and brother Michael. Already, at a young age, he possessed the characteristic ways of "Huckleberry Finn" which is the way he was remembered by childhood friends.

John Ripley's mother, Verna, had a wonderful sense of humor and wore a constant smile, but was also an opinionated Southern lady who never missed the opportunity to remind her Northerner husband that the South had really won the Civil War.

Mary Susan, with the family dog, taught John Ripley (far left) his catechism with the help of her sister Patricia (right). The two of them would sometimes criticize George (second from right) and Michael (far right) for not remembering points of the Faith.

Three generations of Ripleys: (Back row left to right) brothers Joseph Ripley, Dr. Louis Ripley and Francis "Bud" Ripley. (Seated left to right) Grandmother Pauline Droit Ripley, John Ripley, Grandfather Walter Starr Ripley and Verna with Michael Ripley. (Front row left to right) Mary Susan, George and Patricia Ripley.

John Ripley dressed as a sailor and standing at attention—an image of what was to come.

John, perched on the right arm of Verna's chair (right portion of photo), wears his trademark smile of someone who was about to do something, with brother Michael (right). Back row left to right: George, Mary Susan, Patricia, and Bud Ripley.

Francis Droit "Bud" Ripley (left of center), with his friends, was all smiles as a Naval Academy midshipman. His joy was later turned to sorrow when he was expelled for missing his boat in Hawaii.

Michael Ripley (far left) listens attentively while Bud (center left) looks with curiosity as John receives one of his many medals for bravery.

Bud (right), here pictured with Marine Corps legend Chesty Puller, was described as a hero worshiper. Little did Bud know the mark his son would make in the military world.

John Ripley
(right) as a
Naval Academy
midshipman
with his brother
Michael.

Mary Susanna "Sweetsie" Gilmore nestled in her Uncle John's arms
with her brother Clement. "We adored him," she said.

Mickey Runion (left) and John Ripley were inseparable. Mickey went on to fight in Vietnam and was killed in a helicopter crash. Clement Brock perches himself in the middle with a broken arm he got while rough housing with his Uncle John.

"Bud" Ripley (far right) with his three sons who served their country as United States Marines. From left, John, Michael and George.

Castle Island, located in the middle of the New River just behind the Ripley home, was where Mickey Runion and John Ripley spent most of their youth.

The "trestle" where John Ripley would entertain his nephews by hand-walking across the bottom—a curious stunt which he would repeat later in Vietnam.

A smiling John and Moline pass under a canopy of swords outside Saint Jude's Catholic Church in Radford, Virginia. He was a chaste spouse who once said, "I have never been, nor will I ever be unfaithful to my wife."

John Ripley with the British Royal Marines' green beret he had just received. This, the last of four special forces programs he completed, earned him the unique distinction among warriors of *quad body*. Moline keeps a tender and watchful eye on their four-year-old son Stephen.

Colonel Ripley stands tall and proud, on the evening of June 9, 1972, as he receives the Navy Cross from then Secretary of the Navy John Warner

Colonel Ripley with his wife Moline, after receiving the Navy Cross during the evening Parade at the Marine Corps Barracks in Washington D.C.

American Legion Hall where the young John Ripley and his brothers mopped up the beer-soaked floors, so the faithful could attend Mass.

This photo was taken on March 25, 1972. Four days later, those pictured would heroically face the largest North Vietnamese onslaught of the entire war. (From left to right) Captain James Johnson, Captain John Ripley, Lieutenant Colonel Gerald Turley and Captain William Weschmeyer.

Captain John Ripley (far right) as company Commander of a unit that became known as "Ripley's Raiders." He was ferocious in battle, always led from the front and his men loved him.

Diorama depicting John Ripley's exploits in Dong Ha. It is located in Bancroft Hall at the United States Naval Academy in Annapolis, Maryland.

John Ripley (right), standing on a slope near "Mudders ridge," explains Lima Company's recent action to his older brother George (left).

Mary Susan Goodykoontz at her home in Radford, Virginia, standing beside the painting of her brother John Ripley under the Dong Ha Bridge.

John Ripley, the warrior.

This picture, which first appeared in LIFE Magazine, was taken after John Ripley had blown the Dong Ha bridge. In spite of having almost nothing to eat for days, he mustered the energy to chase down this vehicle so that wounded Marines would not be left behind.

Colonel John Ripley in 1992, on the day of his retirement from VMI as Professor of Naval Science. Robert "Loch" Lowman (right) encouraged him to join the Marine Corps and his uncle, Dr. Louis Ripley (left) was, according the Mary Susan Goodykoontz, "his favorite person in the world."

The author (left) with John Ripley outside the Grand Ballroom of the Mayflower Hotel in Washington D.C., after the colonel's speech at the launching of the book: *Nobility and Analogous Traditional Elites in the Allocutions of Pius XII.*

John Ripley with the calm and serious face of an archetypal warrior. One of his favorite sayings from Stonewall Jackson was "press the attack."

Missiles (SAMs), hundreds of artillery pieces and three armored mechanized regiments. Those in Leatherneck Square were facing the largest single massing of NVA soldiers during the entire war.

By Saturday, April 1, the South Vietnamese 3rd Division located in the Ring of Steel was overrun. One regiment simply capitulated and fell back across the Cua Viet River without reporting their dislodgment. This action left those in higher command in the dark as to the troop strength on the front lines. The NVA, seeing the South's weakness, exploited it to the maximum degree and began an unhindered advance towards the Dong Ha Bridge. Once there, they would easily be able to cross the river—or at least that is what they thought—giving them a breakthrough point to the south down Highway 1 through Dong Ha and directly towards Quang Tri city.

What complicated matters even more was that Camp Carroll, located just west of Dong Ha, was in the process of surrendering. This meant that the NVA could proceed towards the bridge virtually unmolested with a convoy of over 200 T-54 and PT-76 Soviet-made tanks. The bridge was the only crossing in the area capable of sustaining such heavy loads.

LIEUTENANT COLONEL
TURLEY PLAYS HIS LAST CARD

Up to this point, Turley had made numerous critical decisions in his newly acquired, even if not so coveted, position as COC Senior Advisor. Seeing the seriousness of their situation, he made the most significant decision during the entire Easter Offensive. He ordered the 3rd ARVN Division to commit its reserve. This happened to be the famed "Soi Bien" or Sea Wolves of the 3rd Vietnamese Marine Corps Battalion, commanded by veteran South Vietnamese Marine Major (now Lieutenant Colonel) Le Ba Binh, and his American counterpart, Captain John Walter Ripley. It was a meager force facing overwhelming odds. Lieutenant Colonel Turley knew that committing his reserve was the equivalent of playing his last card since this was the only remaining infantry battalion, but he was out of options.

It was then that he radioed Captain Ripley on a secure line with strict orders to proceed to the Cua Viet River and destroy the Dong Ha Bridge. One U.S. Marine and his Vietnamese comrades were thus sent into a collision course with a column of 200 enemy tanks now rumbling down Highway 1, 30,000 soldiers and artillery fire from 130mm and 120mm guns that were pounding the South Vietnamese resistance.

Major Binh received equally stark orders, but was undaunted by them. When he heard rumors that Dong Ha had fallen, he called his radio operator over and grabbed the microphone out of his hand. In an angry voice, he bellowed out to all who were listening that as long as there was one Marine left standing, Dong Ha belonged to them.

Ripley then echoed that same message to Lieutenant Colonel Turley.

"We are going to stay here," he said, "and we are going to die here."

Ripley, Binh and Turley knew that it was a seemingly impossible mission which would end in certain death. However, Captain Ripley took a more philosophical approach.

"The idea that I would be able to even finish the job before the enemy got me was ludicrous," he said. "When you know you're not going to make it, a wonderful thing happens: You stop being cluttered by the feeling that you're going to [survive]."[1] Dong Ha was not the first time he had been on the hopeless side of desperation.

---

1. http://ap.google.com/article/ALeqM5gtVtXOzyrVkGYATFuCPzLvNSJXjw D9476EL00.

He would reflect on his experiences there at a later date: "Yet my attitude had always been, no obstacle is too great, too numerous, too hopeless, and as I looked out across that river, I had every reason to feel a little bit concerned about what was there. But there is simply no place for negativism in the life of a Marine."[2] It was for this reason that he obeyed the order to "hold and die" without flinching.

---

2. TFP Lectures.

Painting by Col. Charles Waterhouse of John Ripley dangling above the Cua Viet River as angry North Vietnamese soldiers fire upon him.

Chapter 15
THE DONG HA BRIDGE[1]

*This story is of a few Americans who stood
firm during the most desperate extremes of
combat. They made a difference in a war
in which no one was supposed to make a
difference. They had nowhere to turn and
no hope for help. They did their duty.*
— **Colonel John Ripley**

The intensity of the battle took its toll on Captain Ripley's
battalion but also on the civilian population. The situation he
faced as he gazed at the 60-ton bridge he was ordered to destroy
was best described by eyewitnesses as "chaotic." South
Vietnamese jammed the roads in a frantic attempt to escape the
wrath of the Communist NVA who intentionally targeted those
very roads to kill civilians. Many fell dead and wounded from
enemy fire that came from an aggressor intent on spreading
panic. Mothers clutching crying babies staggered down the
road in zombie-like fashion, followed by shell-shocked children. Thousands of South Vietnamese Marines, seeing the futil-
ity of resistance, threw down their arms, removed their military
insignias and joined the amorphous mass.

As the North Vietnamese continued pounding the South into
submission with seemingly unlimited artillery, it became clear
that they were dead set on crossing the bridge. The only thing
standing in their way at this point was a brave, but battered,
Vietnamese Marine battalion and one lethal U.S. Marine
armed with the know-how to become their worst nightmare.

Colonel Turley recalled visiting John Ripley on the evening

---

1. See Appendix III for an article on the destruction of the Dong Ha Bridge by TFP
author Jeremias Wells. Colonel Ripley considered it to be the most accurate article of
any he had seen describing his actions at the Dong Ha Bridge. The author personally
saw numerous copies of this piece in Colonel Ripley's private file cabinet.

of April 1. As they sat in a makeshift bunker, shells were landing all around them. Their brief conversation was constantly
interrupted by incoming rounds which forced them to take
cover. In spite of the intensity of the situation and the daunting
task that lay ahead of him, Colonel Turley was amazed at how
calm John Ripley was.

Blowing the bridge would not be easy, but his training with the
Army Rangers, Navy Underwater Demolition team and Royal
Marine Special Boat Service (SBS) made him more than quali-
fied to do the job. Shortly before he arrived at the structure
aboard an M-48 tank driven by Major Jim Smock, a South
Vietnamese Marine Sergeant fired upon and disabled one of the
T-54 tanks on the north side of the river. This stopped the whole
column, purchasing John Ripley precious time to do his work.

Both he and Major Smock dismounted their tank under the
cover of an old bunker. They were then forced to run across an
open space under heavy artillery and small arms fire before
arriving at the juncture of the bridge and the approach ramp.
Awaiting their arrival were five Vietnamese army engineers
hiding beneath the foot of the bridge, frightened to death by the
intense incoming fire. Although they had carried over 500 lbs
of TNT and the necessary C-4 explosives under the bridge,
they flatly refused to assist in its destruction. Eventually, all
five faded away, leaving Ripley and Smock completely alone.

RELIVING HIS ADVENTURESOME CHILDHOOD

After surveying the structure, Captain Ripley realized that
to bring it down he would have to place the TNT in a staggered
alignment between the six gigantic girders. This would require
numerous trips into the underbelly of the bridge, each time
pushing wooden crates of TNT between the girders and carrying two 40-lb satchel charges over his shoulders. It also meant
he would have to go deep into the bridge superstructure to

accomplish this task which would bring him closer to enemy fire on the opposite bank.

The scenario before him was hauntingly similar to the Battle of Cloyd's Mountain he knew by heart as a boy. The big difference here was that he was practically alone in the undertaking. Everything depended on him and he did not waste a minute in accomplishing the task. Comparisons to his youth did not end with the history of Radford, but also included one of his favorite boyhood stunts.

To get the TNT into the bridge he had to hand-walk into the structure, a feat that was reminiscent of his "Huckleberry Finn" days. Once again, like he did as a boy under the trestle over the New River, he would walk arm over arm under the bridge, clutching the I-beam girders. Although, this time he would not have enthusiastic nephews egging him on, but angry North Vietnamese trying to kill him.

**"COMMENCE FIRING
IMMEDIATELY AND DON'T STOP"**

What complicated matters was the chain link "sapper" fence strategically placed at the abutment in order to prevent sabotage to the under section of the bridge. On top of the fence was razor-sharp concertina wire. Captain Ripley had to crawl over the top of the concertina and let Smock hand him the explosives. This meant passing through the wire, which shredded his uniform and tore into his flesh. The subsequent loss of blood only increased his fatigue.

His first trip out was a good indication of what the whole ordeal would entail. Grasping the bottom flanges of the I-beam, he began hand-walking. Arriving at the designated spot for the placement of the first satchel charges, he laboriously swung his body back and forth to catapult himself up in-between the girders. The effort sapped his low supply of energy as he dangled precariously above the water 30 feet below. After several attempts, he was finally able to lodge his heels in the I-beams and work his way into the steel where he placed the explosives. He then crawled back to the bank, while still inside the flanges of the I-beams, where Major Smock passed him a crate of dynamite, requiring an equally grueling trip back to the same spot, dragging the 180-lb load. Each time he swung back down out of the steel, Communist NVA on the opposite bank fired at him causing rounds to ricochet all around.

Seeing the intensity of the fire and the possibility that his efforts would be in vain, he radioed for immediate naval gunfire to be placed on the bridge and surrounding enemy position from Captain William Thearle aboard the USS Buchanan, now situated off the coast in the Gulf of Tonkin. Those monitoring the radio calls knew that the situation was desperate. Captain Ripley was actually calling for Buchanan's 5.54-inch guns to fire almost directly on top of his own position. Captain Thearle initially refused this "danger close" mission until he reviewed his tactical maps, since he recognized how close the rounds could come to Americans in the area. John Ripley's response to the delay showed clearly that the fulfillment of the mission was primary, even if it meant his own destruction.

"Commence firing immediately," he said, "and don't stop."

The physical effort and mental concentration required in this effort took such a toll that at one point Captain Ripley passed out under the bridge while straddled between two I-beams. He was jolted to consciousness once again by a 100mm tank round from the disabled T-54 main battle tank, that slammed into the side of the bridge, sending shock waves through his body. The vibrations almost knocked him into the river.

Chapter 16
"JESUS, MARY, GET ME THERE!"

The only way I was going to be
able to do this was simply to ask
God to come along with me.
— **Colonel John Ripley**

Before the completion of the first part of his mission, Captain Ripley had made a dozen trips between the abutment and the underbelly of the bridge. It is one thing for a soldier in the heat of battle to look death in the face and accomplish his mission; what Captain Ripley did was much more. Considering the continual enemy fire, each trip into the bridge was a conscious decision to sacrifice his life. Yet, each time Major Smock squeezed another crate of dynamite through the wire, Ripley pushed his tired body back out into the line of fire and faced death once more in spite of the extreme level of physical exhaustion he was now experiencing.

At one point, he remembered it was Easter Sunday which provoked thoughts of family back home and his children opening their Easter baskets. He denied himself even this comfort since the precise demolition work he was doing demanded total concentration. He could not allow thoughts from home to stir his emotions.

Putting the explosives in place was merely the first part of his heroic undertaking. Now, he would have to go back to set the detonators. Although he would have preferred electrical blasting caps and wire to do the job, none were in sight. He was thus forced to use the old-fashioned percussion caps and primer cord, but here also he ran into an obstacle. The crimpers used to connect percussion caps to primer cord were also missing. Undeterred, he fell back on the field expediency he learned in Army Ranger School. In such circumstances, they were trained to crimp the detonators with their teeth. What stuck out in his mind at that point, however, were the consequences of a single wrong move. This was graphically exemplified by a Ranger instructor illustrating what a blasting cap was capable of doing to a softball. As he crimped the detonators with his teeth, he suppressed the horrifying thought that one wrong move would be sufficient to blow his head off.

DIVINE INTERVENTION

After successfully crimping a sufficient number of caps, he now had to make another trip out into the bridge to set the detonators and time fuse into the plastic explosive. Once he reappeared, the North Vietnamese began firing with even greater intensity than before. Hundreds of rounds whizzed by his body. However, he reached the explosives and lit the end of the time fuse, the length of which he calculated would give him about thirty minutes.

It had taken him over three grueling hours to prepare the bridge for detonation and at this point, he felt his strength fading and feared he might pass out again.

"The only way I was going to be able to do this," he said, "was simply to ask God to come along with me."[1] Marines are able to make it through physically demanding exercises with the use of rhythmic chants. He decided to use his own improvised Catholic version and began a continual prayer of: "Jesus, Mary, get me there!" He said it so loudly that Major Smock, waiting for him on the bank, began repeating the same prayer, perhaps without realizing what it meant.[2]

After making what he thought was his last trip, the exhausted Marine was greeted by a smiling Major Smock. "Look what

1. TFP lectures.
2. John Grider Miller, *The Bridge at Dong Ha* (Annapolis, Md.: United States Naval Institute Press, 1989) p. 126.

I found," he said. Captain Ripley almost fainted upon seeing a box clearly labeled "electrical detonators." It was at this point that the value of the second effort, another of his life lessons, came flooding back.

"You can prepare very well and yet you can fail," he said years later. "It is the second effort… that's what wins." Most men would have called it a day, but he had always been taught to rig a backup charge in case the blasting caps did not work. A return trip would be very different since he now had not only enemy fire to contend with, but also the nagging thought of how much time remained of the 30-minute fuse he had lit. These were the thoughts that ran through his mind as he pulled himself upwards, went through the concertina wire once again and was greeted by a hail of arms fire from his angry opponents on the opposite bank.

After setting the electrical detonators, he returned to Major Smock, alive, but completely exhausted, before mechanically falling to the ground.

DEFENDING THE INNOCENT

After catching his breath, he was back on his feet. With a roll of detonating wire slung over his shoulder, he and Major Smock made their way back to the bunker where they searched for a way to trigger the explosion since they had no blasting box. Some distance away they found an old burned-out jeep with a battery that appeared to be in good condition. In haste, he applied the electrical wire to the battery terminals. Nothing happened! He then switched the wires, expecting any minute to see the bridge go up in smoke. Still nothing, nothing but the terrible thought of failure and a paralyzing fatigue.

As he was waiting for the bridge to explode, he noticed two figures walking down the road towards him. As they got closer, he could make out the desperate scene of a mother who had lost her left foot and was hobbling along on a makeshift splint. She held a baby in her arms and some steps behind was her daughter, a terrified little girl, barely able to keep up. The scene caused Captain Ripley a movement of compassion and fear. Although he was unable to blow the bridge with the electrical rigging, the time fuse was still burning. If the bridge blew, the little girl would certainly not survive the impact.

The man who had singlehandedly faced an opposing army during his trips out into the bridge, the Marine who, in a moment of desperation, had called down naval gunfire on top of himself in an attitude of supreme self-sacrifice, would not sit by and allow an innocent child to perish if he could help it. His spirit of chivalry would not allow it.

Forgetting everything else, he bolted in her direction and scooped her up with one arm while still running. When they had almost reached her mother, the two were lifted off the ground by the explosion of the bridge and thrown through the air before landing on top of a heap of dead bodies on the roadside. The girl landed on top of him, dazed, but alive. As John Ripley looked in the direction of the explosion, all he remembered was seeing massive chunks of concrete and steel spiraling through the air. After coming to her senses, the little girl jumped up and ran off. Seeing her moments later wandering aimlessly along the road, he picked her up again and took her to the nearest house for safety where she was eventually reunited with her mother.

"THE BRIDGE IS DOWN"

He then found his radioman and called Lieutenant Colonel Turley. Without the slightest bit of bravado, he succinctly announced, "Sir, the bridge is down." It was Easter Sunday and the entire South Vietnamese Army, after being beaten down for days, had received their own type of resurrection. While they gave shouts of joy, however, Captain Ripley knew that the battle was not over. A column of NVA tanks and a hornets' nest of angry North Vietnamese wanting revenge were just north of the Cua Viet River. However, the USS Buchanan was just off the coast, ready to send more naval gunfire their way.

Here was Captain Ripley's chance. It was payback time for the North Vietnamese who had wreaked such havoc upon his men and the defenseless South Vietnamese populace. He was just about to call in the big guns again, when he stopped. He remembered the little girl once more and feared for her safety. To destroy enemy tanks that were now log jammed along Highway 1 just north of the river would be an easy task for the Buchanan, but he did not want to risk injuring the little girl in the process. He ran back to the place he had left her and saw two figures walking up the road. It was the injured woman and her daughter. With her safely out of the way, he called for artillery fire, which decimated many of the enemy tanks.

Colonel Turley could not have been more surprised at the successful completion of a mission he was certain would end in Ripley's death. In a later report on the Easter Offensive, he summarized John Ripley's actions in the following way:

> Captain Ripley's success against impossible odds in actually destroying the bridge was an epic struggle in itself. And in a climate of seemingly national policy failure on the Vietnam War, Captain Ripley's destruction of the Dong Ha Bridge and halting the NVA's primary attacking forces was immediately recognized at the National Command Authority (NCA) and Defense Department levels as the single historic event which brought the advancing NVA's multi-division [assault] to a halt on the North side of the Cua Viet River. One man's persistence to com-

plete his mission, his leadership under the most stressful combat conditions and his raw courage made the difference in the hundreds of smaller battles that took place that day. Captain Ripley's indomitable spirit, conspicuous gallantry and intrepidity at the risk of his life was far above "beyond the call of duty," as his actions helped turn the tide of the Easter Offensive 1972. Within hours, his singular destruction of the Dong Ha Bridge was hailed by the U.S. newspaper and television crews on the scene and dispatched back to the United States. Captain Ripley justifiably received international recognition of his heroic act.[3]

Patrick Mooney was a personal friend of Colonel Ripley and now works at the Marine Corps Museum in Quantico, Virginia which John Ripley was instrumental in establishing. He qualified the destruction of the Dong Ha Bridge as an act of heroism on par with the greatest acts of valor in American history.

---

3. Excerpt from Colonel Turley's official account of John Ripley's actions at the Dong Ha Bridge.

Chapter 17
GIAP'S FRUSTRATING END TO A BLOODY STALEMATE

Wars are not won by soldiers who are
merely proper, but by those who are heroes.
— **Plinio Corrêa de Oliveira**

As daring as Captain Ripley's actions had been, the intensity of the battle only increased after the destruction of the Dong Ha Bridge. Ripley's actions were so outstanding, however, that members of high command wanted to recognize his efforts with an appropriate medal. Everything indicated he was worthy of the nation's highest award: the Medal of Honor. A Fast Action Award Report, explained Colonel Turley, was subsequently generated in the field under the most extreme circumstances. However, such a report must be completed within a 48-hour period and interviewing witnesses, in particular Major Jim Smock who saw everything firsthand, was virtually impossible. He and Captain Ripley were still fighting to stay alive and didn't have time for much else.

The intensity of the battle during the Easter Offensive continued for another eight days. Stephen Ripley provided the best description for laymen to understand what his father was enduring at this point of the conflict.

"To get an idea of what that's like," he said, "wake up at 4:00 a.m., take a cold shower with your clothes on. Go outside, run a marathon. Don't have lunch. Roll around in the dirt. Take another cold shower and keep going. Repeat that for 10 days."

General Giap, architect of the Easter Offensive, was persistent. With the coveted Dong Ha Bridge now in pieces at the bottom of the Cua Viet River, his tanks were not able to get across, but his infantry were. Thirty thousand Communist troops were soon reinforced by over 10,000 fresh soldiers who continued to pour across the Cua Viet River. It wasn't long before Camp Carroll, unable to resist, finally surrendered. The attitude of Captain Ripley and the 3rd Battalion, however, remained defiant.

Over the next weeks, opposing forces locked horns on two more occasions. The first occurred on the morning of April 6 at a pagoda just south of Dong Ha, which 3rd Battalion was try-ing to hold. As the North Vietnamese began a fierce mortar attack, a group of American correspondents and cameramen showed up to film the action, not realizing the danger of the sit-uation. Captain Ripley's radio operator was killed during this skirmish and Major Smock was wounded and later evacuated. Ripley continued to fight, but now had to contend with pushy journalists wanting a good picture.

At one point, John Ripley had just loaded two injured Marines onto a personnel carrier and was running to save another when the vehicle began speeding away, slinging mud in its path. A photographer close by captured a prize-winning shot of the hero as he was pursuing the vehicle. The picture was published in *LIFE Magazine*. What was not caught on camera was the rest of the battle that degenerated into hand-to-hand combat.

GENERAL VO NGUYEN GIAP'S DEMISE

Senior U.S. commanders finally realized that the offensive was aimed at Saigon and called for airstrikes. A week later, as American planes bombed Hanoi, South Vietnamese Marines continued their heroic resistance and took refuge in the Quang Tri Citadel. On May 1, the North Vietnamese besieged the feu-dal fortress, forcing Captain Ripley and Lieutenant Colonel Binh to fall back. They eventually established a line of resist-ance outside Quang Tri City. It was here that General Giap's invasion into I CORPS was halted. In over a month of intense fighting, he had only advanced 15 miles at a tremendous cost of life.

The inglorious finish of the Easter Offensive and the demise of General Giap were eloquently described by military historian, Colonel John Grider Miller, in his book, *The Bridge at Dong Ha.*

> The NVA's failure to cross the bridge at Dong Ha had led to a bloody stalemate. In Hanoi, a frustrated North Vietnamese Politburo reviewed the situation. They concluded that Gen. Vo Nguyen Giap—victor over the French at Dien Bien Phu, minister of defense throughout the war with the Americans, and architect of the 1972 Easter Offensive—would have to be removed from power.[1]

General Giap's position as Commander General of the NVA, a post he had held for almost 20 years, would, like the bridge of Dong Ha, go up in smoke. John Ripley was promoted to major and eventually colonel and would go on to receive the Navy Cross for heroism.

"UNCOMMON VALOR"

As impressive as the Dong Ha story is, John Ripley was not well-known outside the Marine Corps for over a decade until the release of Colonel Miller's book. The Naval Academy, through the tireless efforts of classmate Paul Galanti, eventually honored him with a diorama in Memorial Hall depicting his exploits at the bridge and his story is now required reading for every Naval Academy plebe.

---

1. John Grider Miller, p. 180.

During the unveiling ceremony of the diorama, Mr. Galanti wanted to further honor John Ripley. He contacted Colonel Truman Crawford, director of the United States Marine Band, asking him to compose a march for the event. Three weeks later, he got a return call from Crawford asking him if he wanted to hear the first playing of a composition he dubbed: "Ripley at the Bridge." It was a stirring march which began with the first notes of the "Marine's Hymn" which, as Mr. Galanti humorously recalled, got all the Marines to stand up. Then there were some notes from "Anchors Away" because John Ripley was also a midshipman at the Naval Academy, followed by a British slow march honoring his days as a Royal Marine. Recognizing his Southern heritage, strains from "Shenandoah" are sprinkled throughout the song. The last notes of the march are from "When Johnny Comes Marching Home," commemorating his glorious return. Although the music was a big hit with Ripley fans, the title was short-lived. Someone in high command thought it inappropriate to name a march after a living Marine. Colonel Crawford then changed the song's name to "Uncommon Valor."

* * *

In the years following Vietnam, Colonel Ripley remained very busy. He spent three years on the West Coast as a Marine officer instructor at Oregon State University. Upon his return to the East Coast, he took time to further his education at American University in Washington, D.C. where he graduated with a Master's degree in December of 1976. Earlier that year, he lost his father Bud who died of pancreatic cancer on the feast of Saint Joseph at 76 years of age.

Through it all, Colonel Ripley never stopped his physical

training and in 1979, he served another six months in Norway, where he was named the commanding officer of the 1st Battalion, 2nd Marines, 2nd Marine Division. In 1981, he attended the Naval War College in Newport, Rhode Island and was then tapped as the Political-Military Planner and Branch Chief of the Joint Chiefs of Staff.

While his former instructors would have been surprised at his appointment in 1984 as the Director of the English and History Departments at the Naval Academy, those who knew him professionally considered him the perfect man for the job. Stories of his tenure at the Academy are legendary, like his reaction one day when he came into the gymnasium and saw several female midshipmen doing aerobics with one of Jane Fonda's exercise tapes. Paul Galanti described how Ripley ejected the tape from the VCR, then stomped it to pieces. He then looked at the girls and said, "See you in my office at 8:00 in the morning."

"The next day," Mr. Galanti said, "he gave them a one-hour history lesson on who Jane Fonda was," explaining how the actress had supported the communists during the Vietnam war and even visited Hanoi for a photo op with America's enemies. After that, he went to the midshipmen store and found out that they were stocking the tape. Grabbing an arm-load of them, he walked over to the person in charge and said, "get rid of these."

In 1988, he was sent to Okinawa, Japan for a year where he served as the assistant chief of staff for the 3rd Marine Expeditionary Force. Barely had he boarded the plane when his mother was admitted to the hospital for an undiagnosed illness. Days later, she suffered a massive stroke and lingered for a short time before dying on Holy Thursday. She was 80 years old. Two weeks later, his older brother George died of colon cancer at 57.

Following his tour in Okinawa, Colonel Ripley was given

command of the 2nd Marine Regiment. With this appointment, he had held every command billet from Platoon Commander to Regimental Commander.

PASSIONATE PLEA TO GO TO WAR

As Colonel John Ripley's military career was winding down, the United States declared war on Iraq. His son, Lieutenant Stephen Ripley, was called up with his unit. It was more than Colonel Ripley could bear, to see his son going to fight a war he wanted to participate in, but couldn't. At that time, he was the commanding officer of the Navy Marine Corps ROTC unit at VMI. From his office there, he sent a letter with an impassioned plea to a friend, asking his help to be sent overseas.

November 9, 1990

Dear J.

I want to go to Saudi. I don't have to tell you how painful it is sitting here watching everything and not being a part of it. Worse, I know there are hundreds of Marines out there who don't want to be there and would love to trade places with me. I have never missed anything. I volunteered to return to RVN [Republic of North Vietnam] when no one else was going, or found reasons not to go...I would give anything to be back with FMF [Fleet Marine Forces] Marines and in any capacity. I have no career ambitions, not that it would matter, just that I want to be with my Marines again and go out with some dignity...

I hope I am not trading on our friendship but I don't know what else to do. Let me put it simply.

I will go anywhere, anytime with no notice.

It makes no difference what job I'm going for or
what I get when I get there.
I am a threat to no one. I have no hidden agenda; I
just want to go.
...I will pay my own way.
There it is. I am grateful for your consideration. I
know I'm asking for a miracle, but I'll go to my grave
hating myself if I don't.

His passionate plea to engage in combat again was ultimately unheeded. Although at the time it was probably not
clear to Colonel Ripley, there was a providential reason that he
was not sent overseas. The course of events would make it
clear that his warrior spirit was now needed on the cultural battlefields in America more than the war zone in Iraq. He was
about to participate in the premier battle of his life in favor of
the loftiest ideals.

Chapter 18
"A HOLY CRUSADE"

The strong man is not afraid to speak out,
but rather he fears remaining silent.
— **Plinio Corrêa de Oliveira**

When his request to return to combat was denied, Colonel Ripley accepted his fate with tranquility. By then, he had accumulated so many medals that it was hard for him to stand erect because of the amount of hardware that decorated his upper body. However, what really defined him was something much larger than the medals that adorned his chest. It was the chivalrous spirit that burned in his heart. In Vietnam, he had distinguished himself by possessing a rare physical courage. The ferocity with which he defended the village people of Dong Ha would now be unleashed in defense of womanhood in America, giving him the chance to show a higher brand of courage. This all came about when the U.S. Justice Department filed a lawsuit against the Virginia Military Institute, contesting its all-male admissions policy.

This school, so steeped in history and tradition, was the last military college to accept women. Even more noteworthy, is that while the court challenge was pending, Virginia Women's Institute of Leadership opened in Staunton, Virginia to offer a parallel program for women. Yet, instead of making use of it, the architects of change opted to destroy the 150-year-old VMI tradition. Colonel Ripley was then the senior Marine officer and head of the NROTC unit at VMI and would not remain silent.

PREPARING YOUNG MEN FOR COMBAT

At that time, some were arguing that the mission of service academies was not to make young men into warriors. Colonel Ripley spoke forcefully against them. He recalled his days as a midshipman and the various things done at that time to instill "aggressive behavior" in the students. They would run obstacle courses, box, wrestle and play contact sports like football.

His opponents claimed that those things were no longer relevant in the new concept of a military academy that trains the "whole person," focusing more on peace than training for war. Colonel Ripley refuted these pacifist notions by reiterating the purpose of such schools in the first place. The main reason for maintaining the all-male tradition, he pointed out, had to do with the very purpose of service academies: to prepare young men for combat.

His thinking was later explained in testimony before Congress over women in combat. At that time he said, "Obviously, we have an academy to train these warriors and those with the expectation of combat." He continued. "...And if that is not the case, then one must ask the obvious question: Why have an academy?"[1]

BEST ARMOR IN A WOMAN'S ARSENAL: FEMININITY

There was another reason that Colonel Ripley opposed women at schools like VMI: his respect for their integrity and the fear he had that standards would be lowered and compromised to help women succeed. He was convinced that our nation's enemies would not pull their punches when fighting women. His motivation is not hard to understand, considering the moral environment in which he was raised.

The Radford, Virginia all-girls college in the late fifties was a bastion of decency, thanks to Dr. Moffett. The city, itself, saw nothing wrong with her strict rules, because the citizens knew that enforcing them was "the right thing to do."

---

1. For Colonel Ripley's complete congressional testimony against women in combat, see Appendix I.

Colonel Ripley, himself, was an outspoken advocate of single-sex schools and did not shy away from his reasons for being so, when he was named president of the Southern Seminary College for Women. He saw schools, like Southern Seminary, as proper environments to prepare women for the battles of life. The best armor in a woman's arsenal, he reasoned, is her femininity.

"When a woman is firm, but feminine, resolute, yet ladylike," he explained, "oftentimes men don't know how to react."[2] However, he knew that sooner or later women would have to face a world that does not always pay them the proper respect.

"They will know there are injustices out there and wrongs to be righted," he said in their defense. "But you don't have to shove their faces in it [for them] to know it's there. [They] don't have to swim in the filth."[3]

Those who knew him will recognize this forceful language as vintage John Ripley. They will also appreciate the elevation of thought he expressed to a friend regarding his testimony in favor of VMI's all-male tradition. In an unpublished letter, he wrote:

> I have seen the VMI case as a near holy Crusade which no good man of integrity could avoid. The rightness, or conversely, the wrongness, of the issues is so clear, so uncluttered, so perfectly in focus.
>
> You put my testimony in the context of courage, and virtually all others have stated this as well. From the standpoint of having something to lose, and a lot if the Navy sees fit, I suppose this may be so. I have seen courage in many forms, but that which I admire far more than physical courage is moral courage,

---

2. Mel Oberg, "Colonel Takes Command at College," *Richmond Times Dispatch*, July 17, 1992.
3. Ibid.

which I define as the will to stick up for your moral and ethical principles when someone turns up the heat. In my view, it has been the lack of courage on the part of a few political leaders which has resulted in VMI having to defend its more than appropriate admissions policy.

National leaders, it seems to me, have acquiesced, caved in and refused to face down the rampant feminists in their quests to neuterize all our institutions under the holy name of equality. However, as we know, equality does not beget fairness. Nor does it produce a better result once imposed.

THE COWARDICE OF SILENCE

In another letter, he wrote:

> ...What must also be considered, in my view, is that to have done nothing—what I call the cowardice of silence—would have marked me, or anyone, as just that, a coward. Still, I was motivated for an even greater reason which had nothing whatsoever to do with how others may view me. This simple motivation, a powerful one, was because it was the right thing to do.

He then compared his physical courage in Dong Ha to the moral courage he displayed in his VMI testimony. In both instances, he recounted saying to himself:

> You are here alone, and indisputably what you do and say can mean a great deal to a great many people...
> These people rely on you, they are counting on you...

> You are right. This is the right thing to do, nothing
> else matters, not threats, not intimidation. Do it...
> This is a landmark event for me and one that I am
> proud to have been involved with, start to finish.
> Threat, fear, intimidation and adversity are not
> strangers to a Marine; nor, most especially, is truth.
> And no matter what we do—certainly no matter what
> we say—truth will prevail.

He also received numerous letters of support. One came
from a former student who appreciated such spirited defense
by a man who many already considered to be a legend in his
own time.

> I want to thank you for having the fortitude to tes-
> tify in the VMI case in the face of the government's
> attempt to discourage you from telling the truth....As
> a former lawyer and judge, I feel qualified to say that
> you were a very credible and effective witness.

"WOMEN SHOULD BE VAUNTED ON HIGH"

There are those who will look upon Colonel Ripley's desire
to exclude women from all-male military schools as sexist.
The common way of stereotyping such a man is with very
broad brush strokes. "He is just another male chauvinist who
dislikes women and wants them in an inferior position." The
spirit which animated John Ripley, however, was his respect,
not disdain, for women. He did not want them relegated to a
footstool, but rather placed upon a throne.

"The greatest institution in America," Thomas Ripley quoted his father as having said, "is the sanctity of the mother."
She is the center of the family. What led him to say this was
the example he remembered of his grandmother Pauline and

mother Verna, but most especially his wife Moline. "The mother of the American family is a person that should be vaunted on high and should never have to deal with the nasty job of doing the ditch digging of our nation, fighting wars, protecting our country."

Chapter 19
IN DEFENSE OF WOMANHOOD AND FEMININITY

*If we see women as equals on the
battlefield, you can be absolutely certain
that the enemy does not see them as equals.
The minute a woman is captured, she is no
longer a POW, she is a victim and an easy
prey... someone upon whom they can
satisfy themselves and their desires.*
— **Colonel John Ripley**

Colonel Ripley's chivalrous mindset is what drove him to speak out in defense of womanhood when liberal politicians were proposing legislation to allow females in combat. Because of his noble principles, he felt they should be spared the brutality of war that he and other American fighting men were willing and well-equipped to endure. In spite of the harshness of battle and the possibility of being captured, brutally tortured and/or killed, there has never been, nor is there now, a shortage of American men, more than willing to enter those hostile environments. Nevertheless, there were those pushing for women to be given the "equality" to fight alongside men.

The conflict came to a head in 1991, when the law exempting them from combat aviation was repealed. This measure was taken, in large part, because U.S. Representative Pat Schroeder had persuaded fellow politicians that women would only fly in combat aircraft in the U.S. Many people saw this as a "salami tactic." American public opinion would choke if required to swallow the whole salami, so it was fed to them one slice at a time.

It was not long before women were piloting, or riding

aboard, aircraft during combat missions abroad because, it was argued, they were relatively safe inside the cockpit. The logical question which was not being asked was: What happens when the plane crashes and the women aboard are captured?

PAINFUL REVELATIONS OF RHONDA CORNUM

Congressman Schroeder skirted this important question and chose rather to cite the successful combat missions flown by women in the first Persian Gulf War. What the American public did not know at the time was the unfortunate experiences of a flight surgeon named Rhonda Cornum. She happened to be flying one of those missions aboard a Black Hawk helicopter which was shot down on February 27, 1991. She and two others survived the crash, but the severity of her injuries and her 5 foot 6, 110-lb frame made resistance to her captors virtually impossible. For eight days, she suffered the horrors of being a POW and upon her release was grateful to be alive.

This regrettable occurrence could have been prevented if the law excluding women from such missions had not been repealed. Perhaps this is the reason that, simultaneous to the repeal of this law, Congress passed legislation to fund the 1992 Presidential Commission on the Assignment of Women in the Armed Forces. The purpose of this commission was to study the issue further. One cannot underestimate the importance of this commission or Colonel Ripley's involvement in it.

For over a year, Rhonda Cornum said her treatment in captivity was no different than what American male prisoners experienced.[1] It was only during the spring of 1992 that she would tell the rest of the story when she was called before the commission.

Up to this point, she had not yet revealed the degree of phys-

1. Ross McKenzie, "Are Women in Combat What We Want?," *The Richmond Times-Dispatch*, July 14, 1992.

ical abuse she suffered in the hands of her captors. It was only when Elaine Donnelly, with the Center for Military Readiness, asked Mrs. Cornum what kind of abuse she endured, that she admitted being sexually molested. She then provided the sad details of her captivity which, for almost a year, had been withheld for reasons that can only be called political. Since that was the first time the American public heard about her abuse, the presidential commission hearing received national headlines. Feminist critics could not restrain their anger at Mrs. Donnelly for asking the sticky question. They knew that Cornum's testimony would be a setback in their hard-fought battle to gain women the coveted equality to fight alongside men in combat. Mrs. Donnelly was appalled at their tactics.

"For [Rhonda Cornum] to withhold that information for more than a year," said Donnelly, "was putting her personal advocacy above the best interest of the nation." Additionally, the very integrity of American women was at stake. The irony of the circumstances could not be more glaring. While Cornum was being violated in Iraq, American politicians at home were working to repeal the very laws meant to prevent such an atrocity.[2]

APPRECIATION FOR THE "GRACEFUL CONDUCT OF WOMEN"

Abuse of women was the primary concern of Colonel John Ripley when his turn came to testify. On June 26, 1992, he provided testimony before the Presidential Commission on the Assignment of Women in the Armed Forces.

His whole life seemed to be a preparation for the deposition he was about to give. For over 30 years, he had distinguished

---

2. In 1991, female pilot Paula Couglin was awarded $6.7 million in the Tailhook scandal because she was groped by drunken male pilots. The Navy would use her case to promote the assignment of women in combat under the premise that this would cause male pilots to respect women more and harass them less.

himself as an outstanding Marine. Besides his qualifications on the battlefield, he was the consummate Southern gentleman. All of the tools in his arsenal were brought to play in a testimony that was a virtual manifesto of the values which most Americans hold dear.

His statement was as courageous as it was sagacious. He began his comments by framing what he considered to be the central point in the debate. "The issue of women in combat," he explained, "should not be argued from the standpoint of female rights or even desires." Many had argued, and still argue this contentious question on the basis of equality. Colonel Ripley, like a true knight, raised the bar high and called upon the commission and the whole nation to protect "femininity, motherhood, and what we have come to appreciate in Western culture as the graceful conduct of women."

He by no means rested his argument on these noble sentiments, but also cited surveys of the time which indicated that 97% of women did not want to be put in combat situations.

"No, I do not want to be in a combat unit," he quoted them saying, "there is no purpose for me being there." The reason they were even having the debate, he pointed out, was so that a pathetically few number of women could gain a higher rank. Pat Schroeder, herself, was quoted as saying: "combat exclusion doesn't keep women out of combat...it keeps them from promotion in certain areas."[3]

BRUTALITY OF COMBAT

Members of the presidential commission were then treated to a series of jaw-dropping examples of combat situations, leaving no doubt that it is an unsuitable environment for

3. Ted Sampley, "Women Warriors, Can They Hack the Real War," *The U.S. Veteran Dispatch,* Aug/Sept 1996.

women. Colonel Ripley described the horrifying experience of being shot down in a helicopter on two consecutive days and the gruesome task of pulling the wounded and dead from the burning aircraft.

"It took not only brute physical strength," he said, "…it took fighting back overwhelming psychological pressure to continue this grisly work. Removing legs from the cockpit, parts of other bodies, and it took overwhelming…effort to overcome any human's gut visceral instinct to get on that same aircraft, rather than stay behind…while that aircraft full of casualties left, and I did so."

He then described his experience as a company commander during his first tour in Vietnam when he lost his company three times during an 11-month period. Casualties included: 13 lieutenants, three senior corpsmen and an additional 15 corpsmen. He, too, was wounded during this period. He recounted another example of seeing a Marine who was skinned alive and nailed to a tree with bridging spikes. Other details were so unspeakably cruel and vulgar that one is amazed at how original the Vietcong were in mutilating human beings.

Colonel Ripley's main point was not only that combat is extremely brutal, but that our enemies, contrary to what some might think, are not like us. This is especially so where the treatment of women is concerned. That is why he chose to finish his examples with the one that pained him most. It was the story of the captured female during the Gulf War who was raped by her captors. While giving testimony, he chose chivalrously not to mention Rhonda Cornum's name. However, the commission members knew exactly of whom he was speaking, since her disclosure and the horrible details of her abuse were then reverberating across the land. As they were catching their breaths and, one might hope, wiping a tear from their eyes, he then bellowed out, "That is the way they will treat female captives or the female wounded left on the battlefield."

Regarding the facts mentioned in his graphic descriptions, he lamented: "None of this reaches the sanctity and the antiseptic cleanliness of a hearing room. It's only on the battlefield."

"IS THIS WHAT WE WANT FOR OUR WOMEN?"

To those still clinging to the optimistic idea that women would be safe in cockpits, he described what happens when aircrafts collide with the earth. If a woman onboard is captured, she becomes a victim:

> ...Someone upon which they can satisfy themselves and their desires. That is the generally accepted view that our enemy has of the so-called woman warrior.
>
> ...She is now a victim, and made so by the incredible stupidity of those who would permit her to encounter with the enemy. She is no longer protected by our own standards of decency, or the Geneva Convention, which few of our enemies have paid the least bit of attention to. She is no longer protected by the well-wishers and the hand-wringing and the pleas and the prayers of the folks here at home. She is a victim, and she will be treated accordingly.

No one knows where the next war will begin, he continued.

> I can, however, tell you with complete accuracy where [it] will end. It will end in the mud. It will end, as all wars do, with filthy, stinking, slogging, infantrymen moving forward to dislodge the enemy—forcing him from his ground by close combat.
>
> It will end with men dying agonizing, painful

deaths, burdened with extraordinary loads, well past
what they once thought to be the limits of their
endurance, and knowing—always knowing—that
there are those among them who will not see tomorrow's dawn. This is the nature of the battlefield. It has
not changed in centuries and will never change—
leading the rational person to ask: Is this what we
want for our women?

He finished his remarks with a scathing rebuke against those
"self-serving few" looking to achieve a higher rank. "They
demean women" he said, and would "damn them to a hell that
they themselves would never have to suffer, because the
women [sent into combat] would be the junior enlisted." As
always, Colonel Ripley looked out for the underdog and understood that those women speaking most loudly for the right to
fight were doing so to the detriment of those of lesser rank.

* * *

In March of 1993, Colonel Ripley spoke out against women in
combat again, this time in a debate which pitted him and William
F. Buckley, founder of the conservative magazine *National
Review*, against Congressman Pat Schroeder and Air Force
Brigadier General Wilma Vaught. On this occasion, a busload of
his students from Southern Seminary went along to witness their
president's involvement in the heated debate. One can only imagine their surprise when Wilma Vaught not only defended women
in combat, but also saw no problem with pregnant women fighting. "There are women," she affirmed, "who are capable of doing

---

4. Elaine Donnelly, "The Commandant, the Colonel, and 'Making Marines',"
National Review Online, November 04, 2008. http://tank.nationalreview.com/
post/?q=NWExOGI4YjI3MTM5MGJjMTViMGQxZTNmZWIzNTE5MWI=

many things up to a very late period in their pregnancy."[4]

If it is true that a picture is worth a thousand words, a photo of Colonel Ripley in an article[5] on this debate is truly priceless. In it, he is leaning forward towards his opponents like a lion ready to leap. His indignation is truly beautiful, because it is directed against those who defend the ludicrous idea of sending women, even those with child, into the heat of combat.

5. Mark Mattox, "On the 'Firing Line': SVCW Students Travel to Washington to see their President Debate 'Women in Combat Issue'," The News Gazette, March 24, 1993.

Chapter 20
EXPERIMENTS IN A PETRI DISH

Moral courage is the most valuable, and
usually the most absent, characteristic in men.
— **General George Patton**

It was not long before Colonel Ripley would tackle another cultural issue. This one would be even more sensitive than women in combat.

Throughout our nation's history, the American military has taken great pride in its ability to attract and train the finest soldiers in the world. Like any other institution, the military has always set down barriers to those who are incapable of meeting its standards.

In 1993, legislation was introduced before Congress to allow homosexuals to enter the hallowed ranks of the military. Members of Congress debated this issue for months and, in April of that year, Colonel John Ripley stepped forward and voiced his opinion before the House Armed Services Committee.[1]

He began by explaining the wrong idea many people had of the military at that time. Its primary purpose, he argued, was not to be a "disaster relief force, peacekeepers" or "the first line in humanitarian aid in foreign countries." Neither was it a "platform for social engineering." Its purpose for existence, he argued, was fighting wars, "especially violent and protracted warfare on a large, continuous scale."

"In our present role, the Armed Forces have moved away from the traditional role of fighting and winning, into a more bizarre and unintended role as an engine of social change. We have become, in effect, a large petri dish where social laboratories and experimenters can create new systems or grow new models to test..."

---

1. See Appendix II.

SELF-SEEKING OPPORTUNISM

Those infected with this wrong idea began entering the military using terminologies that were totally foreign to Colonel Ripley. Whereas he joined because of idealism, others did so for "career" and "job protection." Those seeking to enter the military arguing about their "rights," "entitlements" and "so-called needs" were "an instant indicator of trouble in combat." Those on the front lines, he argued, understood that in order to win battles, one must sacrifice his own essential needs—even his instinct of self-preservation—for the good of the unit.

"When an individual starts thinking about himself, or permits himself to be distracted by anything, this distraction can ultimately lead to destruction. In combat, if you are distracted, even for an instant, you will get people killed and you will get yourself killed."

Along with unit cohesiveness, another essential element in combat, he argued, is trust.

> No one can trust a leader, nor can a leader trust a subordinate, if they think there are sexual feelings just beneath the surface. It makes no difference if he's suppressing those feelings. It makes trust virtually impossible! Trust is also a function of character and all those elements that make up such character; respect, loyalty... and certainly courage...Men trust each other when they are alike; like values, similar training, the same objectives, the traditional values given to them by their families before they entered the military. This commonality breeds trust; trust in each other, and without this trust there will be no leadership, not on the battlefield, not anywhere.

COVERED IN OTHER MEN'S BLOOD

It is understandable that he argued against the acceptance of homosexuals in the military due to the number of communicable diseases, like AIDS, running rampant in their community.[2]

If those on the court fled from former professional basketball player Magic Johnson[3] because of an open cut, he argued, "imagine how these men in combat will feel when they literally swim in each other's blood during firefights and [the] evacuation of the wounded and dead."

To illustrate this, he told the story of a fellow Marine who was "atomized" right in front of him one day. When he looked around, he and thirty Marines in the vicinity were literally covered in the man's blood. Colonel Ripley, himself, was a living example of the collateral damage which can occur on the battlefield. Up until the time of this testimony, he had enjoyed perfect health and always gave a great deal of importance to physical fitness. In the last years of his life, he endured serious operations and debilitating illnesses which were a consequence of Hepatitis B, a liver-destroying disease he contracted in Vietnam through contact with other men's blood.

"YOU ARE ATTACKING OUR HONOR"

Colonel Ripley finished his impassioned testimony with one last plea to the House Armed Services Committee members, asking them not to change the military which "has fought our nation's wars for over two hundred years...

"I can tell you as a Marine, you will virtually destroy the

---

2. The prevalence of disease in the homosexual community is well documented in: TFP Committee on American Issues, *Defending a Higher Law: Why We Must Resist Same-Sex "Marriage" and the Homosexual Movement* (Spring Grove, Penn.: The American Society for the Defense of Tradition, Family and Property, 2004) pp. 113-114.
3. Magic Johnson was diagnosed with HIV on October 26, 1991 and retired. He later attempted to return to the NBA, but soon after left due to the outcry of the public and his fellow players.

Marine Corps by imposing on us this deviation of values
which we hold dear, which we have fought for and which we
know to be proper. You are attacking our personal integrity,
you are attacking our honor and no military organization can
exist without honor and personal integrity. You are asking us
to look the other way, ignoring a practice we feel deviant,
destructive and in conflict with American and God-fearing
values. We cannot do this.

"I implore you as an American and as a Marine who has
fought for his country and loves his Corps and country more
than life itself, not to lead us into this ambush from which we
can never recover."

After his heroic statement and the tireless efforts of the Center
for Military Readiness, the regulations forbidding homosexuals
in the military were written into law. Unable to strike down this
legislation, the Clinton administration devised a policy
euphemistically dubbed "don't ask, don't tell" and the effect it
had on American public opinion was enormous. Although the
military's policy prohibiting homosexuals did not change, the
public thought it had. The only thing that changed was the exclusion of the question that had always appeared on induction
forms, asking whether or not a new recruit was homosexual.[4]

THE BATTLE CONTINUES

During his testimony, Colonel Ripley informed the panel
about what others in the military thought of this issue, thus

---

4. "In 1996, the U.S. Court of Appeals for the Fourth Circuit looked beyond the
'Don't Ask, Don't Tell' catch-phrase and recognized the difference between Clinton's
policy and the law. In a 9-4 decision that denied the appeal of Navy Lieutenant Paul
G. Thomasson, a professed homosexual who wanted to stay in the Navy, U.S. Circuit
Judge Michael Luttig wrote about the exclusion law: 'Like the pre-1993 [policy], it
codifies [the statute, and] unambiguously prohibits all known homosexuals from
serving in the military . . .'," Elaine Donnelly, "Congress Rejected 'Don't Ask, Don't
Tell'," http://www.cmrlink.org/ HMilitary.asp?docID=298.

showing clearly that he was not alone in his thinking. A TROA (The Retired Officers Association) Gallup Poll of the time indicated that well over 80% of retired officers favored maintaining the integrity of the Armed Forces.

Things have not changed since then. During the writing of this book, the issue of repealing the prohibition of homosexuals in the military has come up again. President Obama, although firm in his intentions to move forward with a repeal of the law, looked into what members of the military thought about the issue. While the proponents of the repeal garnered some signatures, the Center for Military Readiness received an overwhelmingly favorable reaction against the repeal among high-ranking officers.

To date, over 1,150 retired flag and general officers have signed a formal statement to the President and Members of Congress, showing their disapproval for the repeal. The list includes: 51 four-star officers, former Marine Corps Commandant General Carl Mundy and two Medal of Honor Recipients, Generals James Livingston and Patrick H. Brady.

Steering committee members of the group promoting the petition,[5] General James J. Lindsay, Admiral Jerome Johnson, Lieutenant General E. G. Shuler Jr. and General Joseph J. Went (all retired), wrote a stinging op-ed in *The Washington Post* on the issue. Echoing Colonel Ripley's sentiments, they stated that repealing the ban would "weaken our military" and inflict great harm on our all-volunteer force. They cited a recent survey conducted by *Military Times*, in which nearly 10% of respondents said they "would not reenlist or extend their service" if the repeal went through, while 14% said "they would consider terminating their careers after serving their obligated tours."[6]

5. The organization promoting the petition drive is called: The Flag and General Officers for the Military. http://flagandgeneralofficersforthemilitary.com/.
6. Brendan McGarry, "Troops oppose repeal of 'don't ask'," *Military Times*, Dec. 29, 2008.

Chapter 21
TRADITIONAL AMERICAN ELITE

However horrible the incidents of war
may be, the soldier who is called upon to
offer and to give his life for his country is
the noblest development of mankind.
— **General Douglas MacArthur**

After having taken such heroic stances on crucial moral issues of his day, it was only reasonable that later in 1993, Colonel Ripley would be one of the main speakers for the launching of a book dealing with the essential role of leaders in society.

Nobility and Analogous Traditional Elites in the Allocutions of Pius XII, by Professor Plinio Corrêa de Oliveira[1] is a collection of the speeches given by Pope Pius XII to the Roman Patriciate and Nobility over several years. During these meetings, the Holy Father explained the crucial role of the nobility and traditional elites in guiding society down the right path. After addressing the audience of over 800 participants filling the Grand Ballroom at the Mayflower Hotel in downtown Washington, D.C., Colonel Ripley obtained a copy of the book for each member of his family.

A study of nobility is far beyond the scope of this book. What is of importance to our subject is the book's American appendix which clarifies the often confused notion that people have of elites. Many scorn them because of a false concept they have of elites represented by the worldly members of the "jet set," high-priced athletes and glamorous movie stars. According to the principles laid out in *Nobility and Analogous Traditional Elites*, these "false elites" live a life that is "eco-

---

1. Professor Plinio Corrêa de Oliveira is founder of the Brazilian Society for the Defense of Tradition, Family and Property and inspiration for 20 autonomous, sister TFP organizations throughout the world.

nomically and socially disproportionate to their origins or social level."[2]

A true and authentic elite, on the contrary, is one who is not overly concerned about increasing his fame or fortune, but rather dedicates himself to the common good, including the development and appreciation for society's cultural values. His prestige, therefore, comes from his commitment to the nation not the size of his bank account or his popularity.

LIVING UP TO HIS FAMILY NAME

Although Colonel Ripley was not among the monetary elites, he was able to live a life "largely independent of the maxims governing a Revolutionary society, the extravagant styles and the hype of media propaganda."[3]

He not only descended from a line of warriors who had fought in every conflict since the Revolutionary War, including family members that fought for different sides during the Civil War, he also hailed from a signer of the Declaration of Independence. He was proud of the service his forbearers had rendered the country and did everything in his power not to tarnish the name he inherited. This was a motivating factor for his joining the Marines and becoming a distinguished officer.

He also unabashedly practiced the Faith, proving that one can be a very good Marine and a practicing Catholic at the same time. By doing so, he became the high point in a family that had already distinguished itself through public service.

Unlike some leaders of the time that vacillated like weathervanes amidst the cultural storms, he was like a lighthouse, cutting through the clouded issues that were contrary to his upbringing. To the degree that he threw himself into the public spotlight to address controversial issues, he propelled

2. Plinio Corrêa de Oliveira, *Nobility and Analogous Traditional Elites in the Allocutions of Pius XII* (Lanham, Md.: Hamilton Press, 1993) p. 188.
3. Ibid., p. 190.

himself into a much larger role in American society. In so doing, he fulfilled another characteristic of an authentic elite whose mission is to express the true spirit of a nation. The elite elevates himself to a standard above the community and, in so doing, becomes the embodiment of the values it holds dear. Such a man, *Nobility and Analogous Traditional Elites* points out, "will only fulfill his vocation when he has a clear idea of the grandeur of his country and is willing to represent it in his person."[4]

"THE STANDARD TO WHICH WE ALL ASPIRE"

This is what shone through during the politically incorrect, yet sublimely beautiful, testimonies he gave against sending American women into combat. While others paid homage to the "god of equality," he chose to defend the noble ideals of womanhood and femininity. The same was true with the issue of homosexuals in the military. John Ripley saw their admittance as a deviation from values that Marines hold dear and one which attacked their very honor.

By upholding such lofty ideals, he represented, in his very person, the "dream" to which Americans are called. This was evidenced by General Thomas L. Wilkerson, who said of him: "I admired John not only because of his obvious war heroism, but because of how he conducted himself after the war. John was the standard to which we all aspire."[5] The men who served with him in Lima Company affirmed that the influence he had over them went far beyond the battlefield and that "they were better husbands, fathers, and did better in their civilian careers by having been unintentionally exposed to his brand of leadership."[6]

---

4. Ibid., p. 195.
5. http://forums.military.com/eve/forums/a/tpc/f/954191642/m/6210095502001.
6. Richard Botkin, "Honor the Warrior: 'Ripley's Raiders' 40-Year Reunion." http://hughhewitt.townhall.com/blog/g/24e2518b-2104-40c0-9c02-ce3a12fb7a34.

John Solbach, one of "Ripley's Raiders," described him as a person who was not only a model to follow, but one who took an active role in helping those who fought with him.

"He didn't just serve and then go and forget about the people he served with. He sought out his Marines [after the war]. We meant a lot to him. He cultivated us… and took great delight in our accomplishments. He was proud of us, not only for what we did over there, but for what we did since then. He loved his men," Mr. Solbach concluded, "and his men loved him."

* * *

After facing numerous external enemies, he would, during the last decade of his life, face a health issue that would have killed any other man. It might have taken his life also, if it weren't for the assistance of the Marine Corps and a Ranger doctor that just would not quit.

Chapter 22

THE MOST DRAMATIC LIVER TRANSPLANT IN HISTORY

*My entire life has been one of walking
on the edge of a razor blade.*
— Colonel John Ripley

Up until the time of his retirement, Colonel Ripley's health was never an issue. In 1992, he received the alarming news that he had colon cancer, the same disease which killed his brother George. Colonel Ripley's case was so severe, doctors were forced to remove a large section of his colon.

Shortly afterwards, he heard the first tolls of his death knell when his liver began to show signs of wear. This was due, not only to the Hepatitis B which he contracted in Vietnam, but also to a hereditary illness known as Alpha Antitrypsin which also attacks the lungs. In 2001, doctors announced that he had reached a critical state and his liver was deteriorating quickly. He would need a transplant. This was the beginning of one of the last and most dramatic events in his storied life.

"IF 20,000 VIETNAMESE COULDN'T KILL HIM, NEITHER WILL I"

Dr. Cal Matsumoto was assigned to his case and Colonel Ripley could not have hoped for a better physician. He was not just any Army MD. Whereas others joined the Army to be doctors, the only thing some of them have in common with fighting troops is their green uniform. Dr. Matsumoto was different. Besides being an excellent surgeon, he was also, like Colonel Ripley, an Army Ranger, which meant that he was just as proficient in taking lives as he was in saving them. He therefore understood how tough John Ripley was, because they were both part of the same elite group.

Over the next year and a half, Colonel Ripley made frequent visits to the hospital for complications and infections that were clear indicators that his liver was giving out, even if the determined patient was not. In late July 2002, the Ripley family received a much-anticipated phone call that a matching liver was found. Colonel Ripley was subsequently rushed to Georgetown Hospital in Washington, D.C. to receive what he thought would be a life-saving organ.

When Dr. Matsumoto and the rest of the transplant team opened him up, what they found was alarming. Besides the Hepatitis B and the Alpha Antitrypsin, they also found a tumor on his liver which had now become enlarged. His blood pressure had dropped dangerously low and he was suffering from an advanced stage of Portal Vein Thrombosis, which meant the portal vein that provides about 70% percent of the blood to the liver was in a chronic state of clotting. All of this caused Dr. Matsumoto and the rest of the team a great deal of concern. Doing the operation on such a frail patient might be enough to kill him. Not doing the operation would mean certain death. Being an Army Ranger himself, he knew what John Ripley was capable of enduring and proceeded with the transplant. "If 20,000 North Vietnamese couldn't kill Colonel Ripley," he reasoned, "then neither will I." It was with this state of spirit that Dr. Matsumoto began what he thought would be just a difficult transplant.

FIRST LIVER FAILS

After eight hours of surgery, they were able to reroute all of Colonel Ripley's veins to feed the new liver, stitch him up and take him into intensive care. Once there, Dr. Matsumoto pointed to a renal bag and told Thomas and Stephen, who were by their father's side, "That bag needs to fill up every hour. If it is not filling up, we have a problem." After more than an hour, the bag remained empty. Dr. Matsumoto was called in, took one look at the patient and announced the alarming news, "his liver is failing." It was quickly determined that he was suffering from Primary Nonfunction (PNF).

"When a person suffers from PNF," Dr. Matsumoto explained, "the whole body basically shuts down." The jaundice color of Colonel Ripley's skin was a clear indicator that lethal toxins were now poisoning his body and causing severe bloating. He had formerly weighed 175 lbs and now had ballooned to over 400. Colonel Ripley was once again, as he had been in Dong Ha, on the hopeless side of desperation.

The incision in his side had been closed with staples providing a quick opening in the event that his body rejected the first liver. The doctors knew there were only two options for him, obtain another liver or go to the tomb. Dr. Matsumoto wasted no time putting Colonel Ripley back on the transplant list.

His son Thomas kept vigil by his father's side and somehow knew, as did Dr. Matsumoto, that he would pull through. At 7:00 a.m. on July 24, two days after the first transplant, family members received a phone call that another matching liver was found in Philadelphia. What did not match was the time it would take to get it to him. At this point, the doctors were measuring his life by hours, not days. The hospital was unable to obtain a helicopter from an organ transportation agency and the two-and-a-half-hour drive from Philadelphia to Georgetown would only make an already grave problem worse. Most transplant patients literally die waiting for an organ and that was a risk they were not ready to take.

"I had been in situations," said Dr. Matsumoto, "where at the very last minute you get a call [that an organ] was found and everybody is happy. I have never been in a situation where

you had [an organ] but you couldn't get to it in time. It is
unusual for that to happen."

SECOND LIVER RECEIVES
"PRESIDENTIAL TREATMENT"

As Colonel Ripley lay unconscious on his bed with his life
slowly fading, his sons knew there was only one way to get the
liver to him in time. They would have to bring in the Marines.
Thomas Ripley picked up the phone and called General James
L. Jones, Marine Corps Commandant at the time, and informed
him of the situation. They had everything they needed to save
their father's life, except adequate transportation. That phone
call set in motion a series of events, which according to Dr.
Matsumoto, probably made this the most dramatic liver transplant in history.

John Ripley had given 35 glorious years to the Corps and
had never refused a mission, no matter how difficult. He had
distinguished himself on many occasions by going above and
beyond the call of duty. To the Corps it was not just any Marine
dying of a bad liver, it was the passing of a legend and they
were not quite ready to let go.

When Marines take on a mission there is nothing that gets
in their way. The Commandant found a solution by going to the
very top. The liver that would save a Marine Corps hero would
receive "presidential treatment" aboard a CH-46 helicopter.
Normally, this aircraft is used by the Commander in Chief,
with the designation of Marine One. However, this trip was
reserved for the life-saving organ for John Walter Ripley.

Dr. Matsumoto was shocked when Thomas Ripley told him
that they would be riding aboard a Presidential helicopter.
However, they needed to hurry to Anacostia Naval Air Station,
one of the few locations in the vicinity large enough to accommodate such a big bird. The two of them jumped into Dr.

Matsumoto's car. Moments later, as they were making their way towards Anacostia, they realized his car was almost on empty. Stopping for gas was out of the question since the minutes used for this routine task might mean the death of Thomas' father. As they weaved through D.C. traffic, the blinking gas light was a constant reminder that the surgeon designated for this life-saving trip might reach his destination too late.

They finally arrived at the air station with the car running on fumes. Dr. Matsumoto threw his car keys to the closest person and jumped into the helicopter. Before he could get buckled in, the chopper was lifting off.

LAST RITES

Three hours after the initial call that an organ was available, the CH-46 descended upon Philadelphia. Thomas and the doctor were met by an ambulance and a police escort, both provided by a Marine from Philadelphia who had served under Colonel Ripley. The team of doctors were then whisked away with screaming sirens to the hospital where they retrieved the liver. As the doctors returned to the aircraft carrying the coveted organ, Thomas Ripley began to worry.

His older brother Stephen was now beside his unconscious father's bed, keeping him abreast of the situation. The doctors were doing everything they could, but he was fading quickly. The family priest had already administered the Last Rites and now they had something else to worry about. The Georgetown Hospital helipad could not accommodate the huge CH-46 and a landing at Anacostia would mean another circuitous and time-consuming drive through D.C. traffic. In a desperate race against the clock, the two brothers, both retired captains, began removing obstacles in military fashion.

Thomas had a friend who called the president of Georgetown.

Since they could not land on the helipad, why not the football field. A construction crew was quickly summoned and began tearing down fences to make room for the chopper before it was decided that the area was simply too crowded for a safe landing. The brothers then suggested a symbolic location, the patch of lawn in front of the Iwo Jima Memorial. Although it was a beautiful idea, no one seemed to think it would work.

The solution came from yet another Marine, Sergeant Thomas Hardy. He was a Vietnam veteran who went on to become a D.C. helicopter pilot. When asked if he would shuttle the liver from Anacostia to Georgetown with his smaller aircraft, his response was simple.

"This [is] a Marine Corps mission," he said. "Once a Marine, always a Marine."[1]

The liver transplant was ultimately successful thanks to a Ranger doctor who would not give up and practically the entire United States Marine Corps. When asked later by reporters why they spent so much money on one man, General Jones' response was succinct: "He is a living legend."

The operation was successful and, as Colonel Ripley recovered in his room after the surgery, he received an unexpected visit from a Marine Corps Color Guard carrying the hallowed Battle Colors. This is not just any flag. It is adorned with fifty colorful streamers representing the battles Marines have fought in from the Revolutionary War until today. Only two such flags exist. The original is kept at the barracks on 8th and I streets in Washington, D.C., while a duplicate remains in the office of the Commandant of the Marine Corps at the Pentagon.

Normally, the Battle Colors never leave his office, but after seeing Colonel Ripley make such an extraordinary recovery

---

1. Ellen Gamerman, "'*Semper Fidelis*' Saves A Life," *The Baltimore Sun*, August 16, 2002.

from what should have been a life-ending surgery, General Jones made an exception. The flag was delivered to his room with all the pomp one would expect from a Marine Corps ceremony and placed at the foot of the warrior's bed with orders from the Commandant.

"These colors are not to leave this room until you leave the room."

Chapter 23
FINAL NOTES IN
LIFE'S "SYMPHONY"

Old soldiers never die, they just fade away.
— **General Douglas MacArthur**

Colonel Ripley went on to make a full recovery with the constant help of his devoted wife, Moline, who waited on him hand and foot. He endured this battle like so many others in life, with a philosophical approach. He had always noticed that his life was like a symphony where everyone knows "his or her role and plays it to perfection. ... I never could have made it this far without everyone in the symphony."[1] No one played a more important role than Moline. He would now have his last greatest difficulty in life in relation to her.

At the time of his liver transplant, he began to notice that she was suffering alarming signs of memory loss. Her age didn't seem to justify the change. Although he did not want to consider what it might be, the passage of time made it painfully clear that she was suffering from Alzheimer's disease. It was a slow and painful process which began with little things like forgetting her purse and difficulty in completing household tasks, but became progressively worse.

She, who had taken care of him during his serious illnesses, was eventually reduced to a wheelchair and required round-the-clock care. Try as he might, the man who had defeated every enemy on the battlefield was unable to save the person who meant most to him from this debilitating disease. He admitted to family members that his wife's illness was the

---

1. Ross Mackenzie, "A Warrior Departs: Tell Them My Story," *Townhall.com*, November 20, 2008, http://townhall.com/columnists/RossMackenzie/2008/11/20/a_warrior_departs_tell_them_my_story.

most difficult thing he had to endure in his life and his gentility towards her left an impression on all who knew them.

Father Peter McGeory, a personal friend of the family, witnessed a moving scene at a Naval Academy sporting event
which illustrated this point. While everyone was socializing
before the game, someone asked, "Where is Colonel Ripley?"
Then, Father McGeory noticed a Marine on his knees in the far
corner of the room next to a lady in a wheelchair. It was John
Ripley, the warrior, spoon-feeding his severely disabled wife
as he gently spoke to her. It is an image he would never forget.
As Moline's illness progressed, her husband was unable to
give her the care she needed and was forced to find proper
assistance outside the home.

MENTORING

During the next years, he continued to live a very active life,
but never stopped reading.

"Whereas most people have only one book on their night-
stand," Stephen Ripley said, "our father had four or five—and
he read them all." The man who had difficulties in school early
on, continued to live up to the status of a "philosopher" which
some attributed to him.

He also spent a lot of time mentoring midshipmen at the
Naval Academy and anyone in need of his assistance. One day,
while he was attending Mass at the Naval Academy chapel, he
was approached by Father Peter McGeory who was worried
about a midshipman who was a bit depressed. The young man
had gotten into some trouble and was put on restrictions. In
spite of some disciplinary problems, he was otherwise a good
kid and, like Colonel Ripley, he attended Mass on a daily basis.
Father McGeory asked the veteran Marine to speak with the
young man and try to lift his spirits. He was delighted with the
request, since he loved nothing more than to counsel those

beginning their military careers.

He approached the 21-year-old without revealing his identity and proceeded to explain the academic struggles he had while attending the Academy and encouraged the young man to keep trying. After the brief counseling session, Colonel Ripley walked away. The midshipman was impressed by the numerous hardships of the former graduate, but was still unaware of his identity. When Father McGeory informed him that it was John Ripley, the young man was shocked. He, like every other academy student, knew of the Dong Ha Bridge incident, but never imagined he would have the chance to speak personally with such a hero. The brief conversation with a man of such importance was enough to lift his spirits.

Colonel Ripley was also a mentor to Douglas Zembiec who went on to excel in the Marine Corps and earned the rank of major. The man who became known as the "Lion of Fallujah," for his heroics in Iraq, held Colonel Ripley up as one of his heroes and credited him as being one of the greatest influences in his life. In personal journals he kept on leadership, Major Zambiec wrote of values identical to those of John Ripley: "Be a man of principal. Fight for what you believe in. Keep your word. Live with integrity. Be brave. Believe in something bigger than yourself. Serve your country."[2]

Major Zembiec's tenacious style of fighting and the care he showed towards his men also imitated Colonel Ripley, as did the time he took during war to write condolence letters to the families of Marines killed in combat. Before he was sent overseas, he asked Colonel Ripley to inform his wife, Pamela, should something happen to him. Colonel Ripley was forced to

---

2. Gunnery Sergeant Mark Oliva, "Lion of Fallujah Is Laid to Rest," May 19, 2007. http://www.forcerecon.com/Major_Douglas_A_Zembiec.htm.

carry out that painful task in May of 2007 when Zembiec was killed by small arms fire while leading a raid in Baghdad.

EXAMPLE FOR THOSE FIGHTING IN IRAQ

Colonel Ripley's influence extended well beyond the Marine Corps. His example on the battlefield was an inspiration for troops in other branches of the military who fought in recent conflicts. Marvin Johnson of Roanoke, Virginia explained the enormous impact Colonel Ripley had on the Army.

Johnson fought in the second Gulf War in 2004 as a specialist with the Army National Guard. Their main mission was to make sure supplies made it through the main route from southern to central Iraq, thirty miles northwest of Baghdad. One night, before a particularly difficult mission, their commanding officer entered the room before lights out and made an announcement.

"It is reading time," he said. Marvin Johnson, along with nearly every other soldier, pulled out his personal copy of *The Bridge at Dong Ha*. At that time, the book could be purchased on every Marine and Army base in the nation and most everyone had a copy because of the essential core values that Colonel Ripley exemplified.

"Our particular commander thought it was a great book to read for every young soldier going to war because of his courage." Johnson said, "This quality will carry you through the most adverse situations as it did for [Colonel Ripley]."

They spent the next 20 minutes reading about the destruction of the Dong Ha Bridge, before the commander re-entered the room to announce that reading time was over. Before leaving, he dispelled any doubts of those in the room about the difficulty they were to face the following day.

"If you think you are unable to do what we are supposed to do tomorrow," he said, "just look at what [John Ripley] did."

Although he never met Colonel Ripley personally, Mr. Johnson revered him as one of the greatest Marines of all time.

HE SIMPLY FADED AWAY...

Colonel Ripley also spent a good amount of time giving motivational speeches to groups around the country. In late October 2008, he was slated to give two talks to anxious crowds in Pennsylvania and New York.

Two weeks before, he had been in Florida where he watched his youngest son participate in a marathon. John Ripley Jr. said he was proud to finish the race, even if near dead last. One would have never known where he placed by the reaction of his proud father. Colonel Ripley always displayed a boyish enthusiasm at the accomplishments of his children. He was waiting for him at the finish line with his characteristic smile and gave him a pat on the back, as if he had won the race.

On October 27, he hand-delivered a birthday card to his oldest son Stephen at work because he would be going out of town the following day and did not want him to think he had forgotten—a caring father to the end. That evening, he had dinner with friends, one of whom was a member of the elite Navy SEALs. They enjoyed his company and noticed nothing wrong. Why should they? At that point in his life, Colonel Ripley was actually back into normal physical fitness and feeling good. Father McGeory had seen him exercising only days before and described him as "passing by me at a good clip." "Perhaps," Stephen speculates, "he was overdoing it."

When the family received phone calls from the organizers in Pennsylvania saying he had never shown up, they knew something was wrong. Stephen then decided to check on his father at the family home outside the Naval Academy walls and found that he had passed away in his sleep. The official date of death was given as November 1, the Feast of All Saints.

However, every indication is that he died during the night of October 28.

The man most known for blowing up a 60-ton bridge ended up passing away quietly like the old soldier described so eloquently by General Douglas MacArthur. He didn't die...he simply faded away.

Chapter 24
THE BURIAL OF A LEGEND

"In my mind, we came here to thank God
that men like these have lived, rather
than to regret that they have died."
— **General George Patton**

The family and friends of Colonel John Walter Ripley said their final goodbyes during a moving funeral ceremony on November 7, 2008 at the U.S. Naval Academy in Annapolis, Maryland. He was laid to rest with full military honors in a ceremony that left attendees either teary-eyed or speechless. It was the largest funeral that friend Paul Galanti ever recalls seeing, including those of some admirals.

Among the honorary pallbearers were: General Carl E. Mundy, former Commandant of the Marine Corps (Ret.); Lieutenant General Sir Henry Beverly, Commandant General of the British Royal Marines (Ret.); Colonel Wesley Fox, Congressional Medal of Honor recipient USMC (Ret.); Lieutenant General William Keys, USMC (Ret.); General Walt Boomer, USMC (Ret.); Lieutenant Colonel Le Ba Binh (Ret.) who witnessed the destruction of the Dong Ha Bridge; Charles "Chuck" Goggin, Sgt., 1st Plt, Lima Company 3/3, USMC; Jesse Torres Cpl., RTO, Lima Company 3/3, USMC and Commander Paul Galanti USN (Ret.).

As the polished black hearse carrying the hero's body approached the steps of the main chapel, two Marine infantry platoons in dress blue uniforms with rifles and fixed bayonets snapped to attention. Moments later, six more Marines, looking like they were carved out of granite, approached the hearse in a slow cadence and solemnly removed the casket. They then carried it up several flights of steps and gently placed it on a bier in the back of the chapel.

"OUT OF THE DEPTHS, I CRY TO THEE"

The afternoon sun filtering through the stained glass windows illuminated the incense that wafted through the air, creating a blue haze which hovered over the top of the flag-draped coffin.

As everyone entered that blue haze, in an atmosphere that was truly ethereal, they saw a sea of 2,500 mourners, many of whom were forced to stand for the entire Mass. Row after row of Academy midshipmen, dressed in formal attire, filled the balconies above, while military officers, adorned with medals of gold and silver, sat in the pews below. As the coffin was brought forward, the Naval Academy choir intoned the mournful and soul-stirring lines of the *De Profundis*: "Out of the depths, I cry unto thee, O Lord." The plaintive chant was originally composed as an appeal on the part of the disincarnate soul pleading for mercy before the throne of God. On this day, it produced an atmosphere of added grandeur considering the stature of the man whose funeral Mass was now commencing: a man who the Commandant of the Marine Corps, General James Conway compared to Marine Corp legends Joe Foss and Chesty Puller.

"We were honored to know an authentic Marine Corps legend," he told the audience in a moving eulogy. General Conway then defined John Ripley as a "commander, a mentor, a friend" and a "consummate Southern gentleman."

"John was direct," he said, "and you didn't need to ask him something if you couldn't stand the answer." A good example of this was the heroic testimony Colonel Ripley gave against sending women into combat. Regarding that issue, the Commandant quoted Colonel Ripley as having said, "There are sheep and there are wolves and the wolves always win. So in the end political correctness has no place on the battlefield. There are generations of young Marine officers out there today," he continued, "defending this country with that thought process in mind."

After the Commandant finished his remarks, the choir intoned the "Marine's Hymn." The audience joined in and the words never seemed so meaningful, since they defined Colonel Ripley so well. "We fight our country's battles...for freedom...and to keep our honor clean."

SUBLIME SYMBOLISM

At the conclusion of the funeral Mass, the mourners followed behind the coffin as the body of Colonel Ripley made one last trip across the academy grounds to the cemetery a mile away. The Marine Corps band, playing a military cadence, and two infantry platoons led the way, followed by the hearse, the immediate family and friends. Midshipmen, who were unable to participate because of classes, stood at attention and gave one last salute.

As the coffin was put into place over its final resting place, the sorrowful crowd looked over their shoulders at what sounded like a plane taking off from a nearby airport. As the sound grew louder, four Harriers in a missing man formation flew directly over the flag-draped coffin. While the audience experienced a prideful chill, Thomas Ripley choked back tears of gratitude for the enormous tribute on behalf of the United States Marines.

He was unaware that his father would receive such an honor and explained the deeper meaning behind the gesture. It was in recognition of Colonel Ripley's older brother, Michael, who died while test flying the Harrier. It was one of the many symbolically beautiful gestures witnessed during the day, one Ripley hero honoring another.

As the band played the "Marine's Hymn" off in the distance, mourners witnessed several unique aspects of Marine burials. While every other branch of the Armed Forces uses eight body bearers to carry the coffins of the deceased, the Marine Corps prides itself in using only six. Unlike the other branches, who carry the coffin at waist level, Marines carry their dead at chest level.

After the flyover of the Harriers, mourners witnessed one more thing that makes Marine burials special. In a display of extraordinary strength, the six Marine body bearers raised the coffin of Colonel Ripley to chin level as a final symbol of respect to a fellow Marine.

FINAL FAREWELLS

After lowering the coffin, the body bearers slowly grasped the American flag and pulled it taut over the top of the coffin, while Father McGeory said the final prayers for the soul of Colonel John Ripley and sprinkled the coffin with Holy Water. The grave-like silence which had descended upon the audience was briefly interrupted by the traditional 3-volley salute. During wartime, the three shots were a sign that the casualties were taken care of and fighting could resume.

The sad conclusion to the burial was the moment when the six Marines ceremoniously folded the American flag and presented it to John Ripley's only daughter, Mary—yet another gesture of thanks on behalf of a grateful nation.

Next, everyone was invited to a reception, yet few wanted to leave the gravesite. Many chose to remain close to the polished cherry wood coffin, and a number of fighting men took the opportunity to give one final salute. Some kissed the eagle inlaid in the top, while others exhibited an almost inconsolable emotion.

Lieutenant Colonel Binh approached the bier and placed both hands on the coffin, as if seeking one final support from the man who fought so hard for his people. Overcome by grief, he mechanically fell to his knees, embraced the casket and wept profusely.

"You are no doubt moved by the remembrance of what Colonel Ripley did for your country," Lieutenant Colonel Binh was asked. Being a man of few words, he simply nodded his head in mournful recognition as his eyes welled up with tears.

Before leaving the burial, a Marine lingered who had been at the wake the night before. His demeanor was strikingly humble, yet his upright posture and the glow of admiration in his eyes seemed to indicate a firm determination to follow in the footsteps of a Marine Corps hero. His disposition was not unique. The same look was visible on the face of Naval Academy students who had attentively followed every eulogy of this great man. While mourning the passing of such a legend, they were consoled by the thought that his example will inspire generations to come.

Chapter 25
HE HONORED US ALL

Great men are not those who are only
interested in great things. They are
those who know how to recognize vast
horizons in small things as well.
— **Plinio Corrêa de Oliveira**

There is, perhaps, no better example in America of a person who embodied the principles of the medieval knight, captured so well in the Marine Corps commercials of the eighties, than John Walter Ripley. Just like the knights of old, he lived by a code of honor that was inviolable. In military matters, he was one of the most skilled warriors of his day, having more trigger time than most of his contemporaries.

In war, he took special care to defend those who were unable to defend themselves. He sacrificed himself for the Vietnamese who were resisting an oppressive Communist regime. This is what led him to weep openly during a public lecture, when he reflected on the fact that his heroics in Dong Ha had helped children in a Vietnamese orphanage escape the bloody massacres unleashed by the Communist North Vietnamese during the Easter Offensive. Although he had seen the worst side of human nature and the most violent aspect of war, he never lost a tender side capable of caring for the "little ones."

He was concerned about the family of a Vietnamese farmer, whose pigs his men wanted to shoot. When the Dong Ha Bridge was reduced to rubble, his first thought was not about his own safety, but that of a terrorized little Vietnamese girl who was unable to take care of herself. This tender solicitude for the weak and defenseless was an essential characteristic of the medieval knight, but one that is often overlooked when exhibited by a Marine like Colonel Ripley.

This was the secret, not only to his physical courage during battle, but of his moral courage as a civilian. When the nation contemplated sending women into combat, his voice was a clarion call in opposition. He had seen the horrors of war and could not fathom women being subjected to them. Such a stance required great moral courage. It meant opposing politically correct ideas in vogue at the time. However, this did not deter him from speaking the truth.

GENTLEMAN, WARRIOR AND SCHOLAR

Every man is, to some degree, influenced and motivated by an archetype or the person he strives most to emulate. Colonel Ripley lived like a true Southern gentleman and medieval knight. His style of bravery and honor were not a replication of the medieval style, but were distinctly American and particularly Southern. Although he was proficient in the art of war and used the most modern means to carry it out, many compared him to his personal hero, General Stonewall Jackson. He seldom sent a note to a friend or autographed a picture without including a famous phrase from the great general, such as "Press the Attack." He read almost every book that exists on General Jackson and imitated his tenacious style of doing battle.

He also revered Generals Robert E. Lee and Jeb Stuart and his home in Annapolis, Maryland is a veritable shrine dedicated to these great men of the South. The walls are adorned with their pictures, while the shelves are full of books about their deeds. He had read every one of them and knew these Southerners' style of battle and way of living by heart.

The colonel's personal friend Patrick Mooney, who wept upon hearing the news of Colonel Ripley's untimely death, most accurately described him as a "gentleman, warrior and scholar, who lived in the present and looked to the past in order to better understand the future." Mr. Mooney had the privilege, on numerous occasions, to visit historic battlefields with the late warrior. He was amazed at his knowledge of the great battles fought by American soldiers, and never tired of hearing him tell the details.

"When he spoke, it was like music and the subject matter he spoke about came alive," he said. "He was the 'high priest' and greatest exponent and representative of Marine Corps history; one who lived and breathed history."

It was logical that when John Ripley decided to join the military as a boy, he chose the Marine Corps, not because he had seen an expressive commercial, like the ones described above, but because he was attracted by an archetype. He watched the way Marines returning from the Korean War carried themselves and said, "I want to be like them." Once that decision was made, he never looked back.

When he finally became a Marine Corps warrior, he did not do so like an uncultured Rambo who indiscriminately destroys the world around him because of a personal insult, but as a refined and elegant Marine Corps officer. Although he attained the rank of colonel, many senior officers lament that he was never promoted to general. Others said he could have easily been Commandant of the Corps and many who know of his feats in Dong Ha remain perplexed that his Navy Cross was never upgraded to the Medal of Honor.

STERLING SILVER ROSARY

Colonel Ripley lived in a century of cynicism but maintained an almost childlike innocence. He treasured everything that was given to him. Objects which might seem insignificant to others held a great importance in his life because of their symbolic value. Those who knew him have seen the three bullets which almost took his life. He carried them in his pocket on a safety pin. Whenever he was having a bad day, he would look at them to gain perspective.

What most people do not know is that he shined those bullets and the safety pin to which they were attached. They were symbolic of God's Providence which provided him the opportunity to fight one more day and he was grateful for another chance.

This love of symbolism is what drove him to honor his brother Michael, who died tragically while test flying the Harrier. The family grieved his loss and the fact that his remains had not been found. John Ripley knew the exact location where his brother had crashed and asked his sister, Mary Susan, for something to throw into the water, something meaningful and symbolic. She unselfishly gave him the sterling silver rosary she had received from her godparents at her graduation. He was delighted. It could not have been a more appropriate object, considering the devotion which their family had to the Mother of God. With rosary in hand, he was flown in a helicopter over the exact spot where Michael's plane went down and he dropped the beads into the water. Days later, Michael Ripley's body was recovered and given a Catholic burial.

POETIC AND HISTORICAL VISION

At an early age, Colonel Ripley realized that the struggles of life do not have to tarnish the symbolic beauty that exists in the world, and he never missed an opportunity to admire that beauty. When he was enduring subzero temperatures in northern Norway as a Royal Marine, he overlooked his own physical discomfort to comment on his surroundings.

"The stark beauty of the snow and the mountains in the gray light of night," he said, "is unforgettable."[1] When he had the chance to visit Iwo Jima, he described it as a place "immortalized in our national consciousness for as long as

---

1.   Mel Jeffries, "Radford Man Finds Beauty and Danger in Arctic Land," *Radford News Journal*, March 18, 1970.

there is an America."[2] This unique historical vision shone through on another occasion, when he wrote about a commonly overlooked incident that occurred during the Civil War battle of Chancellorsville, where Stonewall Jackson was killed. As much as he admired his hero, he preferred to recognize an underdog in words that were as poetic as they were historically precise.

The event we should remember about that battle, he affirmed, happened in a "beautifully wooded glen known as Catherine's Furnace." As Jackson's column approached this area, with its turn in the road, they were spotted by the numerically superior army of General Joseph Hooker. Seeing the danger that lie ahead, Stonewall stripped the 23rd Georgian regiment, commanded by Emory Best, from his leading brigade and told them to hold that ground. "Very simple instructions," Colonel Ripley said, "clearly given, quickly understood, and unhesitatingly obeyed."

General Jackson's army continued unmolested as Colonel Emory Best and his brave men struggled against an army that was thirty times larger than their own. At the end of the day, every man was either killed, seriously wounded or captured.

Colonel Ripley concluded:

> No monument to Colonel Emory Best and his Georgians exists at this remote spot. Perhaps no monument to those gallant men exists anywhere except in the hearts of their loved ones.
>
> Nevertheless, we should go to this shaded grove, where arching trees contain the beauty of the forest—its peaceable sounds, its vibrant life; where our ancestors gave their last full measure—where they fought and

---

2. Ross Mackenzie, "A Warrior Departs: Tell Them My Story," *Townhall.com*, November 20, 2008, http://townhall.com/columnists/RossMackenzie/2008/11/20/a_warrior_departs_tell_them_my_story.

died desperately in a forlorn spot: pleasant and remote, and rarely visited. We should place flowers where their lives drained from them entering into the history—and legend—of a nation. We should go to praise, to weep, to bond with simple men who were asked to do the impossible—and who by their efforts honored us all.

*   *   *

During the process of writing this book, I visited Catherine's Furnace and found Colonel Ripley's description of its beauty to be amazingly accurate. After spending a brief time contemplating the events that took place there, I could not help but think more of the heroics of Colonel Ripley than those of the Georgians.

After getting into my car for an hour-and-a-half drive to Annapolis, Maryland, the final resting place of this great man, my reflections on his life were abruptly interrupted by a falcon that swooped down in front of my car. After briefly flying in front of me, it soared off into the distance. The awesome sight reminded me of the values I appreciated in Colonel John Ripley. Most especially, I valued his keen vision that allowed him to see what was most important in life, as well as his ability to rise above the petty interests of the majority of men in the modern world.

I eventually arrived at his grave in the midst of the rolling hills, winding streams and shady trees of the Naval Academy Cemetery. It has a beauty similar to the place where the Georgians died heroically. It is a place like Catherine's Furnace where we should go to place flowers. It is a place to praise and to weep in honor of a man who, during the course of his life, was "asked to do the impossible" and who, by doing so, "honored us all."

ACKNOWLEDGEMENTS

Since gratitude is one of the most fragile of virtues, I wish to recognize and thank all of those who made this work possible.

First of all, I am profoundly indebted to Professor Plinio Corrêa de Oliveira. Before I ever dreamed of picking up a pen, he suggested that I write. He was my mentor, is my model and taught me to admire men like Colonel Ripley.

I thank Colonel John Walter Ripley, himself, for his dedication to our country, the example he gave for all Americans to follow and his friendship, but most especially for living a life worthy of a book. *Semper Fi!* I feel moved to recognize also his wife Moline, a gracious southern lady, who passed away as this book was going to print. May they both rest in peace.

I am also grateful to their children: Stephen, Mary, Thomas and John. One month after their father's death they allowed me into their lives. They graciously granted interviews during a mournful time which should have been theirs alone. They did so because they saw, as I did, the necessity for their father's story to be accurately told. In doing so, they showed a great confidence in me and I only hope that this work lives up to their expectations. Without the photos they provided, stories of life inside the home they shared and free access to Colonel Ripley's private files, this work would not have been possible.

Mrs. Mary Susan Goodykoontz likewise shared invaluable information about her youngest brother's early life. From her I learned, through numerous phone interviews and private conversations, stories of a little boy dubbed "Baby Buck." I will cherish the days I spent with her when she recreated the musical Ripley evenings of old. While she played the piano, I got the unique chance to sing the very same ballads that captured the imagination of John Walter Ripley and slept in the bedroom he occupied when home on visits. In a very short time, I grew to love Colonel Ripley's last living sibling and am honored for the singular privilege to know her.

I thank the people of Radford, Virginia who took the time for interviews to share what they remembered of John Ripley. Among them I am particularly grateful to the men who gather for daily coffee at Wade's Grocery store, but most especially Jim Graham, Robert "Lock" Lowman and his lovely wife Shirley, Danny Jett—childhood friend of Radford's "Huckleberry Finn"—and Don Shomette, a good Marine and a great Catholic.

I would like to recognize Elaine Donnelly of the Center for Military Readiness in gratitude for her assistance in this work and her efforts on behalf of our Armed Forces.

I am also grateful to the many great men and warriors I had the pleasure to meet while doing research for this book:

General James Livingston, USMC (Ret.) and Colonel Wesley L. Fox, USMC (Ret.) who share the distinction of being United States Marines and Medal of Honor recipients. It was truly humbling to speak with men of such caliber and their willing collaboration on this project, while a tribute to Colonel Ripley, was also a great honor for me. I thank Colonel Gerald Turley, another hero of Dong Ha, for granting me a personal interview which left me spellbound and graciously provided yet more priceless details of the destruction of the Dong Ha Bridge that are not commonly known. Commander Paul Galanti, USN (Ret.) provided an interview and priceless stories about John Ripley at the Naval Academy. The men of "Ripley's Raiders" and other Marines granted interviews and much needed assistance to understand John Ripley: the warrior. I express my gratitude most especially to John Solbach, Steven Moore, Ron Darden, Jesse Torres, Eddie McCourt and Patrick Mooney. Richard Botkin, author of *Ride the Thunder*, was always willing to share notes and manuscripts of his work. Along with this invaluable material, I appreciate his encouragement along the way. May God bless all of them for their service to our country.

My special thanks go out to Colonel John Grider Miller who died as this book was going to layout. His encouraging words were a great moral support early on in this undertaking. The lunch we shared only days before his passing and his willingness to review this work were most appreciated. In a relatively short amount of time, I grew very close to this fine Marine, historian and author. I offer my sincere condolences to his wife Susan.

Lastly, and most especially, I thank every single member of the American Society for the Defense of Tradition, Family and Property (TFP) who shared my enthusiasm for one of the great American heroes of our time. The idea of writing this book was truly a dream that seemed impossible. They all helped make this dream a reality. I have no words to thank them.

Norman Fulkerson
Spring Grove, Penn.
September 8, 2009
Feast of the Nativity of the Blessed Virgin Mary

Appendix I
PRESIDENTIAL COMMISSION ON THE ASSIGNMENT OF WOMEN IN THE ARMED FORCES, WASHINGTON, D.C.

Testimony of Colonel John W. Ripley
26 June 1992

COLONEL RIPLEY: I, too, would like to begin with pre-pared remarks.

Ladies and gentlemen of the Commission, I'll start with my background. Very briefly, my association with combat. I served my first combat tour as a young Marine captain company commander of a rifle company for a year in Vietnam, along the DMZ; from Khe Sanh, virtually all of the fire bases, over to the Tonkin Gulf, Con-Tien, Rockpile, Khe Sanh and the jungles in between.

My next tour was with the Vietnamese Marines four years later, where I served in virtually the same area. At the time, Khe Sanh was abandoned, and I had the distinction of being the last American there, having been shot down there twice on two consecutive days.

I also served a tour with the British Royal Marines, where I commanded a rifle company in 4/5 Commando, deployed with them to the Arctic for two years—correction, two winters—and during that same tour, I deployed to Malaya, where I served with the 1st of the 2nd Gurka Rifles and 40 Commando on a post-and-station tour that, to my surprise, in the jungles of northern Malaya, also included combat. I wasn't supposed to know that.

I had been trained exceedingly well by the Marine Corps. I am one of two Marines who have completed all four schools preparatory to reconnaissance training; airborne, scuba, jump, trained with the Navy SEALs at the time they were not SEALs, they were UDT, and, finally, the British Royal Marine Commando Course. There are only two present active-duty Marines so designated.

I give you this information simply to acquaint you with my background and also to say that I feel I have some degree of expertise in this subject, although I personally do not like the term "expert."

During my tenure as a company commander in Vietnam, my company was lost three times over. At the time, my rifle company weighed out at about 210 Marines; 212 perhaps. When you added your attachments, your engineers, scout dogs, and others that joined that company, it could be perhaps another 25, 30 Marines in addition.

I lost my company 300 percent in that 11 months, killed and wounded: 13 lieutenants killed, all my corpsmen, three senior corpsmen and an additional 15 corpsmen, killed and wounded.

(5:34 p.m.)

COLONEL RIPLEY (Continuing): I feel I have a basis upon which to comment, and I would like to read this statement:

First of all, this subject should not be argued from the standpoint of gender differences. It should not be argued from the standpoint of female rights or even desires.

As important as these issues are, I think they pale in the light of the protection of femininity, motherhood, and what we have come to appreciate in Western culture as the graceful conduct of women.

We simply do not want our women to fight. We simply do not want them to be subjected to the indescribable, unless you have been there, the horrors of the battlefield.

The oft-intoned surveys that we have heard have yet to

show you even a reasonable minority of women who feel that they belong in combat units. Survey after survey and question after question, ad nauseam, is answered with the overwhelming majority, around 97 percent, with "No, I do not want to be in a combat unit. There is no purpose for me being there," and the only purpose which has been stated, as we know, is for that pathetically few who strive to gain higher command and feel that they must have served in a combat unit to achieve command, or perhaps higher rank.

The issue then becomes, "I want to be in a combat unit or to serve in that unit, to serve in combat, to qualify myself for promotion," and this, I must tell you, is the worst possible reason, because it is self-serving. It is self-aggrandizing. The only purpose is to further the interest of the individual, as opposed to improving the unit.

Now, combat Marines will tell you that any leader, junior or senior, who focuses on himself, as opposed to the good of the unit, is completely worthless as a leader and he will never be followed willingly, and he will never gain the respect of his Marines.

Combat Marines will also tell you that they distrust any leader who puts his own wellbeing and his own ambition ahead of the mission of the unit, or the good of the unit. And that, ladies and gentlemen, is precisely what is happening here. These extraordinarily few would-be generals are saying, "It is more important for me to be in a combat unit, so that, I may profit from that and become promoted than it is for the unit to be combat effective, combat ready, and successful in combat." And that is precisely what they are saying. That's exactly what this issue is. (It comes down to, "My ambition, my personal needs, are greater than the effectiveness of the unit or the wellbeing and the welfare of my Marines.")

I think that is the issue to be decided. You must ask yourself, then, "Should we permit this aberration of good sense, of logic and the good of the unit? Must we permit that in order to permit an extraordinarily few to become generals and admirals, as they would wish to be?"

I cannot comment to you accurately, or even with experience, on whether a woman would be an effective pilot in combat, never having been a pilot myself. I will tell you at the same time, having been shot down in a helicopter at Khe Sanh on two consecutive days, different aircraft, that no woman could have sustained the crash of the aircraft or the physical effort necessary after the crash to evacuate myself and another 16 dead and wounded in order to remove myself from this combat necessity. No woman could have done that.

No woman remaining alive after such an event would have had the physical power to extract those killed and wounded men; the pilots and the crew, absolutely no one. To see them effectively out of this enemy sanctuary, with no friendlies around me, while I remained behind, I don't think any of them would have done that, would have been physically able to do that, and if in fact they had chosen to do that.

It took not only brute physical strength, pulling man after man out of the aircraft and into another, it took fighting back overwhelming psychological pressure to continue this grisly work, removing legs from the cockpit, parts of other bodies, and it took overwhelming—overwhelming—effort to overcome any human's gut visceral instinct to get on that same aircraft, rather than stay behind, as the only person, while that aircraft full of casualties left; and I did so.

Now, I won't tell you that women do not have courage. Every single mother has courage. I will not tell you that women do not have strength. Women have strength beyond description, and certainly strength of character. I will tell you, however, that this combination of strength, courage, and the suppression of emotion that is required on a daily, perhaps hourly, basis on the battlefield is rare indeed, rare in the species, and is not normally found in the female.

Now, does that offend you? I'm sorry. This is simply an observation. Can women fight? Yes, they can. Can they fight in the conditions of the battlefield of which I am familiar, and the cohesiveness of the unit, and can they add to that cohesiveness? I don't think so. Should they do this? Hell, no! Never.

What is the purpose of it? Why should they? For the self-aggrandizement of a few? Less than one-half of one percent who want to climb this ladder of promotion, is that a good reason, good enough to send our daughters, our sisters, our mothers off to the stinking filth of ground combat? And if you think so—and when I say "you," I refer to the American public—if you think so, then you're different from me. God knows, you're different from me.

If you think women have a so-to-speak right to grovel in this filth, to live in it just because someone above them, senior to them, wants to be promoted, then, my God, what has happened to the American character and the classical idea, western idea, of womanhood?

And some would say, "Well, we'll try this. We'll try to do this. We'll see if it works. We'll experiment." Well, if you do that, then a part of your experiment—no small part—will be the guaranteed, absolutely certain deaths of men and women in mixed-gender units simply because they are there. Thus, the men and women as units in which they are intermixed become completely ineffective on the battlefield, and in fact invite attack and destruction by the enemy, knowing that these are mixed-gender units.

Is it any surprise, as we knew would happen—all of us knew this—that a captured female in the Gulf War was raped, sodomized and violated by her captors? Does that come as a surprise to anyone?

Those that permitted this to happen, who sent her on that mission, should be themselves admonished, if not court-martialed, because that is the way the enemy sees women in combat; all of our enemies. And that is why they will treat—that is the way they will treat female captives or the female wounded left on the battlefield. That is precisely what will happen to them. We know that. We have seen the enemy (combat veterans).

I have seen the enemy, and I know what they do to Marines. They skin them alive—one of my compatriots at Con-Tien— nail them to trees. I've seen that, with bridging spikes.

None of this gets reported. None of this reaches the sanctity and the antiseptic cleanliness of a hearing room. It's only on the battlefield. None of this is chosen to report. This is what happens on the battlefield. This is reality. The picture of a man's privates cut off and stuffed in his mouth, or his fingers cut off so they can pull his rings off, and other unspeakable atrocities. I've seen this. No pictures are ever taken of that. They are never shown. And if they are taken, no one is interested. But that's a regular, not unusual, event in ground combat. That is regular.

Now, admittedly, this doesn't happen in the cockpit. The cockpit is relatively clean. But it damn sure happens when the cockpit collides with the earth, is no longer airborne, and it is suddenly exposed to the enemy. We have seen that. We know that. We have already heard testimony to that.

A great majority of our wars are with enemies that come from societies where women are not valued as equals, and in many cases have no value whatsoever, other than the procreation of warriors. Is that a shocking fact or statement? Well, it shouldn't be. Americans tend to look at other countries and other peoples with the naive statement that: "Oh, they're just like us." Well, they're not just like us. They're completely different from us, and we are seeing this more and more, particularly as our once greatest adversary (Russia) now reputedly is no longer so.

They have very little value for human life—why else would the Soviets have kept our own prisoners?—particularly on the battlefield, and they have almost zero value for females. Females are many times, if not mostly, seen as the pleasurable accompaniment, meant for the pleasure and the sustainment of the men who are actually doing the fighting. And that has taken place in our history, all of our lifetimes.

In a group of prisoners I captured near Khe Sanh, about a dozen enemy, one was a woman. We put them in a compound and we guarded them. They forced her apart, and then during the night—this is all North Vietnamese—they stripped her of absolutely everything, including the rations she was given. The next morning we found her without a stitch of clothing or any other possession, nearly frozen to death, and she was forced not to share in what little sustenance we had given all of the prisoners. They didn't care about her. They cared about themselves.

If we see women as equals on the battlefield, you can be absolutely certain that the enemy do not see them as equals. They see them as victims. The minute a woman is captured, she is no longer a POW; she is a victim and an easy prey, and is someone upon which they can satisfy themselves and their desires. That is the generally accepted view that our enemy has of the so-called woman warrior.

Think back to the prisoners in the Philippines who were captured by the Japanese, which was referred to earlier today.

When that airplane, with its female pilot, returns to earth or collides with earth or she must bail out of it, she is no longer a female pilot; she is now a victim, and made so by the incredible stupidity of those who would permit her to encounter with the enemy. She is no longer protected by our own standards of decency, or the Geneva Convention, which few of our enemies have paid the least bit of attention to. She is no longer protected by the well-wishers and the hand-wringing and the pleas and the prayers of the folks here at home. She is a victim, and she will be treated accordingly.

We have just seen this, for God's sake, in the Gulf War.

I have known many prisoners of war. Last year a Marine was to have been sent to me as my executive officer, who was a prisoner of war for not even two weeks in the Gulf War, he called me and said, "Colonel, I'm sorry to report that I simply cannot come to you as your executive officer, no matter how exciting or enjoyable this duty is. My mind is not right. I must be close to a hospital. I cannot deal with reality. I cannot accept the responsibility for the development of young officer candidates, or even for my own actions." And that for less than a month in a POW camp with an enemy I dare say more tolerant than the enemy in North Vietnam.

I'll take this uniform off in a week, a uniform which I have worn with great pride now, first issued to me 35 years ago, and that will be, for me, a sad day. However, nothing compares with the sadness that I and thousands of other Marines will feel knowing that the sure loss of combat effectiveness in our units will take place if women are introduced into them; profound sadness and equally profound shock. And all for the wrong reason. We don't need them in our combat units. We don't want them in our combat units. And they don't want to be in our combat units. And, as I have said, they have told you this over and over, not this commission. They have said, "don't put us in your combat units," the exception being those self-serving few who would achieve higher rank in their own view.

People who do this do not respect women. They demean

women. They would damn them to a hell that they themselves would never have to suffer, because the women who do this would be the junior enlisteds.

I'll stop my comments there.

COMMISSIONER DONNELLY: Thank you, Colonel Ripley, for your very graphic testimony. We have heard several times in the last couple of days that when we have training regimens, that it is okay to have gender-norming, different standards for physical fitness, because there are physical differences between men and women.

And I know—well, the Naval Academy honors you with a display there. I didn't see it, but I understand that there is, and you are one of the most famous graduates, and you know that, as at the other service academies, this idea of having dual standards is very much reality.

The question to you is, do you think that should continue—if the combat training is not done at the Naval Academy, I have been told, "When, it's done somewhere else," [*sic*] but is there a dissonance there? Should it not be continuous? Do you think it should be continuous, or do you think it is okay to have one kind of training regimen and dual standards for just combat support, and then a different set of standards for direct combat or combat MOSs?

COLONEL RIPLEY: I'll preface my comments by saying that I am on one extreme, I think—it's rather obvious—and that is I feel that the training for ground combat must be as intensive and as physically demanding as it can possibly be, which likens it to the reality of ground combat.

I think it would be impractical for the Naval Academy, or perhaps any other institution at the undergraduate or pre-specialty level, to have that same degree of demand, certainly the physical demand, if not the emotional demand, in all of its students.

I would also say that the changing of standards, the oft-used term "gender-norming," is in fact a depreciation. You are reducing your standards. You're not "norming" your standards; you're lowering your standards. It's a simple fact. If your standards were at one time, as was the case with Tom Draude and myself at the Naval Academy, to perform certain numbers of physical activities, push-ups, pull-ups, boxing, wrestling, the obstacle course, et cetera, et cetera, and then suddenly that changes, and it changes down, then you have lowered your standards. Call it what it is, you have lowered your standards.

Does that answer the question?

COMMISSIONER DONNELLY: Yes, it does, but do you think it is possible to have—you said it would be impractical at the Naval Academy to have a single standard. Is that what you mean?

COLONEL RIPLEY: I think it is impractical to have for combat training the same standards. However, I think that, failing that, there are still great requirements, certainly physical requirements, which males should be held to that females cannot be held to.

That does not mean that females, by their presence, should lower the overall standards for the group. I think it is okay—and I saw this—to have different standards for males and females, rather than this so-called norming process that West Point uses.

COMMISSIONER DONNELLY: Do you think that the standards, then, would be lowered if women were put into combat MOSs, or the attempt was made to have them?

COLONEL RIPLEY: There can't be any question of that.

COMMISSIONER DONNELLY: No question of that?

COLONEL RIPLEY: I think the fact is that you must know. I'll give you an example. We found out when we were told to put women in drill teams—I think this was during the Ford or the Carter Administration; I can't remember which—that we had to remove the operating rod springs in our weapons because women could not come to inspection of arms. They couldn't. The spring has a nine-pound release, and they couldn't move the rifle bolt to the rear.

There are simple physical, psychological, physiological differences that would require this different standard.

Do I feel, if I infer from your question, that this is correct? No, I don't. There are certain limitations on weapons and weapons systems that are essential; that cannot be changed. You reduce the operating rod spring, you make a weapon lighter—the M-16 is a perfect example—it becomes ineffective. We couldn't use the bayonet on the M-16 because the barrel was so light it would bend the barrel. We have corrected that in the Marine Corps. We now have a much heavier barrel, and we increased the buffer spring tension.

A woman cannot pull the cocking handle on a 50-caliber machine gun. She cannot feed a round into the weapon. They cannot undo a hatch, as a man can; the closure grip on a simple hatch. That's a tank hatch or a hatch in a submarine. It can't be done without assistance. Should that be changed? Personally, I don't think so. I think these were designed with the ergonomics and the human application at some point, considerably earlier, and we found these weapons systems to work perfectly. They are certainly rugged, and they should be.

Weapons of today are nowhere near the ruggedness of the M-1 Garrand, just by way of example. That's not to say they are not good weapons, but they are designed with this ruggedness as a factor and, as such, they are more effective. If it is necessary to change it, I think we have derogated the overall effectiveness of the weapon.

COMMSSIONER MOSKOS: Thank you very much.

Colonel Ripley, it was very fascinating about your story and testimony, in addition to the details, the graphic details.

We've been getting mixed signals, you know, from Marine Corps representatives on this question. I wondered if you wanted to comment on that. And my final remark, tying in with that one, is would you draw—where would you draw the lines in the Marines on women's roles, period?

COLONEL RIPLEY: My first answer, sir, is I've got nothing to lose. And that isn't meant to sound the least bit derogatory to those who perhaps do have something to lose. I have spoken very candidly my whole life, and this is an issue too important to hide behind personal concerns. It's just too important.

And I'm not sure who gave you mixed signals, but I feel deep in my heart that anyone who has shared the experiences that I have—and I certainly am not the only one to have done that—feels virtually the same way I do; I can guarantee that—who has had ground combat at the company level for over two years.

Where I would draw the line? I would draw the line at any unit which is required by the mission and the nature of that unit to close with and to kill the enemy by close combat. That includes, in the Marine Corps, rough guess, about 75 percent of all of our combat Marines, all our Marines, and perhaps units; however you define that.

I would say nothing in a Marine division at the regimental level, or those units which are supporting those regiments, the infantry and the artillery regiment.

I would say nothing in combat support units which may find themselves in enemy areas, and that includes, by the way, truck drivers who happen to be carrying essentials from place to place. (6:10 p.m.)

COLONEL RIPLEY (Continuing): In one particular ambush on the 21st of September—correction, 7th of September, many years ago, we had a 100 percent ambush, and the drivers were pulled out of their trucks and were flayed, if you know that term, and they were pinned to their vehicles and left to be there in agony as we closed to try to rescue them.

Combat is combat. Maybe I should begin with my definition of combat, which seems to be a widely diverging definition. Combat suggests combat, to com-bat (verb) someone.

It is an overt, aggressive act. It is not passively awaiting something to happen in a risk environment.

Exposure to combat is not combat. If it were, then we could define a garbage man as someone who performs in combat. Last year I think over 300 garbage men were lost as they fell off their trucks or got compacted in the trash. That's twice the number that we lost in the Gulf War!

So exposure to combat is not combat, not at the infantry level. Combat suggests aggressive, violent behavior—violent behavior—and the satisfaction, the enjoyment that derives from this behavior, that is an essential part of combat, at least among Marines.

Take, for example, linebackers. Linebackers love to crunch somebody. They get a big kick out of knocking not the player down, but anyone down. There is a satisfaction derived from this sort of aggressive behavior. It is common in males. I'm not saying 100 percent, but it is common. And someone can probably define that by chemical balances, testosterone and all the other things. I'm not sure what causes it, but I can tell you it is common. And if it isn't common, this man will never be a good Marine. We don't want him.

Combat suggests this type of aggressive, violent behavior which begets some degree of satisfaction from having encountered and crushed the enemy, a good feeling, a feeling of victory, a wash of emotion. There is something good about this.

I do not subscribe to this feeling that we hate to fight, we don't like to fight, somebody's got to do it. We did it, and we enjoyed it. That did not mean that we would like to be there or that we were warmongers or we necessarily promoted the fact that we were there. We sure as hell didn't. But we got an enormous amount of pleasure out of taking the fight to the enemy and ruining him in the process. That is combat.

It is not exposure to risk. If it were, then call it "risk." Don't call it combat. It's a totally different thing. We put it under the amalgam, this generic term of combat, sitting in a barracks somewhere which is hit by a rocket, and we call that "combat." That's not combat. Combat is an aggressive act, the operative term. You must go after the enemy, you must go for his jugular, and you must enjoy doing it, at least to the point of requiring you to do it again without deriving some emotional hangup therefrom.

I'm sorry, sir, I forgot the rest of your question.

COMMISSIONER O'BEIRNE: Thank you. Colonel Ripley, I would like to ask you a general question about unit cohesion, which we have been discussing quite a bit here at the Commission. We have had at least some fighter pilots, for example, express some hesitation about flying with women making the—expressing the concern that they would be unable to treat a woman comrade the same as they could a male comrade, and we have had infantry, males in the infantry, express the same hesitation.

Based on your experience in supervising the training of these young men—on the other hand, we have been told that they could be trained out of that attitude, that if they trained enough together as either fighter pilots or as infantry troops, they would come to see one another as comrades and, over time, would not treat—males would not find themselves treating females any differently.

Based on your respective lengthy experience, do you think young men, either pilots or infantry troops, could over time be trained to treat female comrades the same as males?

COLONEL RIPLEY: I would say to you yes, absolutely yes, the fact that the females would be in a ground combat unit, infantry battalion, the men would, without question, resent it, it would destroy cohesion, wreck the unit. It would in fact set up not just a dual standard but a grossly unfair standard, because males already accommodate females. They accommodate the fact that females must have certain differences. They must have separate and better, by the nature of them, quarters. The quarters for females are private. They have better head facilities. They have better—just many better things, separate messing facilities in the desert, separate—a lot of things. We accommodate that. We don't necessarily dislike it, but we understand why it is necessary.

If you did that in an infantry battalion, which must, of nature, reduce itself to the lowest denominator, meaning all personnel in that battalion, officer, enlisted, staff non-commissioned officer—everyone has to do the same thing. You dig your own hole, you fetch your own chow, you deal with your own personal hygiene, you: accommodate or you take whatever—share whatever lack of resources there happen to be, they would resent the fact, over a period of time, that the females must have their portion of water or whatever. And it would take a very short period of time that this accommodation which we now do would wear very thin, and it would turn to resentment, gross resentment.

I could give examples of that.

And I would also say that the mere fact that females would be in this unit would not, so to speak, equalize certain actions. The females would never carry the radios. The females would never be sent alone on an LP at night, the most unloved job in the whole unit. The females would never be required to do the things that the males are required to do, of nature, and expected.

No female would ever walk the point; simply would not. I dare say the men would not—would feel very uncomfortable with a female on point.

No female would be required in an emergency situation to move and get another couple of cans of link (machine gun ammunition) or more grenades.

No female would ever carry the outer ring of the base plate, which we don't even have anymore.

No female would be expected to run a landline between your unit and an outpost.

No female would be required to carry "Peter and the Wolf," a dead Marine, which only two male Marines can do, slung on a pole, because that's the only way you can carry them in the jungle.

No female would be required to do 90 percent of the things with which I am familiar, simply because, in many cases, men would not stand for it. They would never, never permit a woman to do the things that they do, of nature, disliking, but

they know they must do it.
I can tell you that unit cohesion would be destroyed.

COMMISSIONER WHITE: [Yes, the first question is for both of you to respond to, and then I have a follow-up question for Colonel Ripley.]
We have been told that part of the reason we need to seriously consider the further integration of women into the military, into combat positions, is because we need the best that there is, and that we can't afford to overlook a segment of the population that may have skills that would be helpful to complete the military's mission. I would like to know if you think that the current operational effectiveness of your particular branch of the service is lacking because we have not reviewed the active-duty women that are willing or desire those positions? Are we operating at decreased effectiveness?

COLONEL RIPLEY: I'll answer first by—I'd like to address this to perhaps those who haven't read my statement on women in ground combat. The issue of American females in combat should first be approached from the standpoint of need, simple need. Using the Vietnam War as a model, we can use the following analysis—and this, by the way, draws on figures from the Veterans Administration—8.7 million men served on active duty during the Vietnam era, 8.7 million, and that was from March '64 to January '73.
Now, of that 8.7 million, 3.4 million served in the Southeast Asia theater, which consisted of the surrounding countries of Thailand, Laos, Cambodia, as well as, of course, the water and the air space surrounding them. By the way, that is only eight percent—that 3.4 million is only eight percent of all men eligible for the draft during that time—eight percent. Ninety-two percent of the men eligible for the draft

were doing something else.

Now, 2.6 million of the 3.4 million who could consider themselves Vietnam veterans, just having been some place in Southeast Asia—2.6 million served in Vietnam, that is, under the threat of enemy action—in the country—2.6 million.

As you can see, I am rapidly going down. Only one in five—one in five of the 2.6 million—fought in combat in a ground combat role, perhaps a half a million, less than a million, a half a million, and two in five provided close combat support, either frequent or infrequent; roughly one million.

Now, I can also tell you that a good figure of 30 percent of those, of that half a million, really never fought in combat, certainly not sustained combat. And I will postulate that that number, the 30 percent, they never saw it because the nature of war is such that squads, platoons and companies did an overwhelming majority of the fighting, whereas the combat support and the combat service support personnel were essentially confined to fire bases which supported those ground combat units, the squads, the platoons, the companies.

The exceptions were in the large-unit actions later in the war, after 1966, late '66, along the DMZ, and the hazardous movement, the very hazardous movement, going between combat bases for resupply and so forth, subject to enemy action.

So we can finally conclude that, at most, there were 350,000 men who saw ground combat on a regular basis in Vietnam, from my original figure of 8.7 million, 3.4 million, and 2.6 million.

The need, therefore, for women to serve in ground combat in any unit, or to augment those units, does not exist. We are not losing a very exceedingly valuable asset by not having women in our combat units.

COMMISSIONER WHITE: I would like to ask two other

questions. Colonel Ripley, you had mentioned earlier that you don't have anything to lose in discussing this issue. Was that just for yourself, or have you heard talk, or are you aware of other people that are concerned or might have reservations about expressing their gut reactions to this issue?

COLONEL RIPLEY: I've heard nothing whatsoever. These are my personal opinions. I'm on a very remote outpost. I rarely get to see my friends in the Marine Corps. I should turn that statement around and say I have a lot to gain, too, rather than nothing to lose. I have an awful lot to gain by, as I stated earlier, protecting American womanhood, if that is not too gratuitous a statement.

COMMISSIONER WHITE: If I could direct one more question at Colonel Ripley, you are a graduate of the Naval Academy, and I visited there in late April and discovered that they seem to be on a mission now of, as they put it, dispelling the "myth" that their mission is to train men to lead other men in combat, or to train warriors, that it has broadened into kind of training the whole person, and one person even said that we shouldn't even be thinking so much about training for war but that we should be thinking more about peace and so forth, and that they are trying to get away from the so-called myth.

I wonder, have you observed any changes in the style of teaching or the attitudes promoted there, or the manner of instruction since your days at the Naval Academy?

COLONEL RIPLEY: I left the Naval Academy five years ago as the senior Marine. At that time, I was living under the same myth, and this so-called myth was up until that time, for 30-some years of my association with the Naval Academy, beginning as a midshipmen, it was a well-understood fact, and it was stated as such, certainly in the statements, the policy statements by the Academy, right up until my service there, leaving in 1987, and certainly that was engendered and spoken publicly by innumerable guest speakers that came to the Naval Academy.

It was only when I read in *The Navy Times*, I think about a year-and-a-half ago, before the present Superintendent's arrival, that the previous Superintendent did not want any more guest speakers to talk about combat—experiences in combat— did not value the experiences themselves, and thought they were not necessarily productive for young midshipmen, and gave the wrong opinion; gave the wrong attitude. It was demeaning for those who would not end up in combat. That's the first I had ever heard of that.

The various things we did there to train, (when I was a midshipman) to instill this aggressive behavior I referred to earlier, they (this new Superintendent) questioned whether that was important anymore. The running of the O-course, (obstacle course) for example, became "irrelevant." It was no longer "relevant" to run the O-course. It was no longer relevant to have boxing and wrestling, aggressive type sports, contact sports.

A wag, a friend of mine, said, "well, if that is the case, why don't we just do away with football? Maybe that is too aggressive!" And although that is not meant to be necessarily humorous, it does bear certain introspection. Why not do away with anything whatsoever that suggests aggressive—aggression or aggressive behavior?

So the issue of whether the Academy exists, or any academies exist, to train so-called warriors or those prepared for their ultimate duty in a combat environment, that issue, to me, should never even be voiced. Obviously, we have an academy to train these warriors, and those with the expectation of combat and service in a combat environment, in whatever capacity, service support or combat support—obviously.

And if that is not the case, then one must ask the obvious question: Why have an academy?

Appendix II
STATEMENT BY
COLONEL JOHN W. RIPLEY, USMC
FOR THE HOUSE ARMED
SERVICES COMMITTEE

THE PRESERVATION OF THE
BAN OF HOMOSEXUALS IN
THE ARMED FORCES

4 May 1993

The American public has been deluded into a false understanding of the real purpose of its military forces. More specifically, it sees the Armed Forces of the nation in a multi-faceted
role; as peacekeepers, as primary disaster relief forces, as the
nation's first line of humanitarian aid in foreign countries, as
well as in our own country; as an enormously successful and
proven platform for social engineering; and as vigilant, obedi-
ent and receptive organizations eagerly prepared to do what its
nation expects of it. The very last thing the citizens of this
nation expect of the military in our particular climate is its single purpose for existence; the fighting and the prosecution of
war; especially violent and protracted warfare on a large, continuous scale. Americans simply don't see us that way anymore. They have seen us in these other roles so often and so
successful that the American mind is conditioned to their military as a helpful, sensitive organization as opposed to a fighting, brutally efficient means of destroying the nation's enemies; and together with that, the expansion of our national policy through this means. In our present role the Armed Forces
have moved away from the traditional role of fighting and win-

ning into a more bizarre and unintended role as an engine of social change. We have become, in effect, a large petri-dish where social laboratories and experimenters can create new systems or grow new models to test, if you will, within a highly controlled group, that which they wish to create.

In the Armed Forces today, you hear such things as, "the rights of the individual," "career path," "job protection" or "constitutionally protected freedoms," which in my youth and later as a senior officer I never heard, ever, any discussion of these subjects. We are and were simply the protectors of these freedoms and never did we have the full embodiment thereof, nor did we expect to enjoy the full embodiment of constitutional freedoms. To even think in these terms as a military man is patently ludicrous and counterproductive to the mindset of a warrior who must think only of mission accomplishment and the good of the unit. Never, ever may he think of his own personal wellbeing in this context.

Our freedoms and our protection come from you, the Congress. From no one else.

You are statutorily and constitutionally required to raise, to provide and to maintain us and you also establish the policies under which we in the Armed Forces function. Let me stress that again. You maintain us and you protect us. We cannot protect ourselves. We cannot, as is the case in other forms of government, close ourselves off from society, establish our own rules and expect to isolate and self-govern. You must do that; you must do that for us.

Not to do that is an abrogation of the sacred trust which we feel in the Armed Forces with you, the Congress, as protectors. As long as I've been a Marine, over thirty-five years, I have known and felt very deeply seated within me the extraordinary lengths the Congress went to, to protect and to look after the Marine Corps. One could even say that the Marine Corps exists today in its modern form because of the National Security Act of 1947 which, in fact, protected and created the modern-day Marine Corps. While in those days other services and certainly the administration were trying to diminish; in fact, do away with, the Marine Corps. So it is to you, the Congress, that we look for overview and for benevolent protection which we personally cannot do ourselves.

In the spirit of this understanding I must ask you, how is it that you can suggest anything that would knowingly from all indications, certainly from the overwhelming majority of opinions of the American public, if not the overwhelming majority here in the Congress, and certainly amongst the military itself (a percentage well over 3/4 in the 80 to 90 percentile range) how could you do anything that would have such a threat of destroying our effectiveness, indeed destroying us altogether as would be the case in lifting the ban of homosexuals in our ranks?

As you know, and as has been said here over and over, service in the military is a privilege extended only to those who are fit and physically able to perform military service. We in the military are very discriminatory. We have always been, and it must be so. We discriminate between the too weak, the too tall, the too fat, the flat-footed, the disease ridden, single parents, morally corrupt, drug users, alcoholics, or abusers of any substance; we discriminate against the altogether good Americans who simply can't be expected to perform at our standards— and our standards are high and obviously must remain high. To serve in the military is a privilege which must be guarded and lived up to every single day by the individual. It is no good to enter the military and having entered then quit.

Your performance must be at an exceptional level in order to remain; to be reenlisted and to be promoted. Perhaps the greatest discrimination of all we practice is perhaps eliminating from our ranks, by way of promotion or separation, those who do not have the ability to proceed on.

Let's talk about leaders for a moment. Especially combat leadership, of which I have had a considerable amount of experience; mostly at the Company and Battalion level. All Marines understand that to win in combat, and to keep focused on the mission, you have to subordinate, to subjugate individual instinct for self-preservation—and for personal protection or comfort—to the needs of the unit. The unit prevails. It is only the unit which you must consider. The unit, it's preservation, and of course the mission. Nothing else matters. When an individual starts thinking about himself, or permits himself to be distracted by anything, this distraction can ultimately lead to destruction. In combat, if you are distracted, even for an instant you will get people killed and you will get yourself killed.

Homosexuals constantly focus on themselves; their so-called needs, what they want, their entitlements, their rights; they never talk about the good of the unit. It is this constant focus on themselves; the inability to subjugate or to subordinate their own personal desire for the good of the unit; this is an instant indicator of trouble in combat; and frankly, even not in combat.

Combat leadership is based exclusively and almost totally on trust. The unit commander, the platoon commander, the company commander must trust in his Marines doing what is expected of them; what they have been trained to do despite the great threat to them. And the Marines trust in their commanders; that they will look after them and get them out of this mess—provide good judgment, good command calls and not expose them unnecessarily to enemy threat.

When sexuality enters the equation, these bonds of trust are simply blown away. No one can trust a leader, nor can a leader trust a subordinate, if they think there are sexual feelings just beneath the surface. It makes no difference if he's suppressing those feelings, it makes trust virtually impossible! Trust is also a function of character and all those elements that make up such character; respect, loyalty up and down, and certainly courage, and the ability to make good judgments. Men trust each other when they are alike; like values, similar training, the same objectives, the traditional values given to them by their families before they entered the military. This commonality breeds trust; trust in each other, and without this trust there will be no leadership—not on the battlefield, not anywhere.

If there is one overwhelming characteristic of the battlefield with which I am familiar, it is the extreme and constant likelihood of death, serious injury, traumatic wounds, torn, bleeding bodies, seen so shocking, that no one in this room could hardly prepare [*sic*] or imagine them. Even realizing that this happens on a frequent, almost daily basis, the combat veteran is still shocked at what he sees when his own men suffer such grievous injuries regularly. Consider the great fear that all military men, in or out of combat, would have knowing that homosexuals serve with them who comprise at least 2/3 of all current AIDS cases and are far more likely to suffer from and spread infectious diseases such as hepatitis, and syphilis than any other group. We see each of them as infectious and life-threatening disease carriers. They are eleven times more probable of having syphilis, they are eight times more probable of having hepatitis and they are a shocking, incredible, five thousand times more probable of having AIDS. How can any sane person not feel threatened working around such an obvious, extraordinary threat to his personal health. And in combat, the story becomes radicalized on a comparison with noncombat.

This is where blood flows so freely that it is unusual throughout the day not to be wearing someone else's blood. Let me give you an example, (the example of the shoot down at Khe Sanh). It seemed to me in combat that on a regular basis, several times a day, I was pinching off someone's artery, sticking a thumb in a chest hole to prevent loss of breath, giving mouth to mouth resuscitation, pouring a canteen of water into an open abdomen to flush out the filth and blood and try to find the wound, trying to gently put a man's jaw back into place so he wouldn't choke to death on his own blood, replacing eyes back in their sockets, collecting limbs and throwing them in ponchos so that they could be evacuated with the body. This was regular activity, normal activity not unusual at all.

Now can you imagine the extraordinary fear fighting men have thinking that at least some of that blood may come from a homosexual who without question to our way of thinking will carry a life threatening disease? I myself carry a very serious disease because of having been immersed in the blood of those around me. I am disabled because of this and it came from normal circumstances not those imposed on me by the forced perversion of homosexuals being around me.

For a homosexual to claim that they are just like the rest of us and that this won't affect them and they will be, so to speak, "clean" is bloody nonsense. We know they have hundreds of sexual partners during their lifetime and they continue to engage in male-to-male sex not using condoms with no thought of the spread of disease. Another realization recently is that they are far more likely to suffer from intestinal disorders, known as gay bowel syndrome. To think that these walking repositories of disease this alone would be imposed on the battlefield—is beyond shocking and virtually defies any logic whatsoever.

No one, no one in this room, no one outside this room, no one anywhere can challenge the logic of not putting that kind of added threat in a combat environment. This could be a threat equal to the enemy itself. A great threat upon the health and the continuing existence of your own men. If Magic Johnson's teammates run from him on the basketball court because he has a open bleeding cut, can you imagine how these men in combat will feel when they literally swim in each other's blood during fire fights and evacuation of the wounded and dead. I don't think you can imagine that because I dare say none of you have experienced it—not to that degree.

But I will tell you this, men will not do this! If you impose that in combat, on us, men will not look after each other. I can tell you that as firmly as I sit here—men will not look after a bleeding, known homosexual; they will not care for him, they will not give him mouth to mouth resuscitation or any other form of aid if in fact it means they are threatening their own life. This will not happen. If you impose this on us you are asking too much. Men under fire will throw themselves on grenades to protect the rest, they will charge ahead of the others to silence a machine gun knowing it will more than likely kill them; they will protect each other from enemy fire under greatly hazardous conditions; but they will not, openly, expose themselves to deadly diseases just because the individual himself is irresponsible and has contracted such a disease. That will not happen. You cannot ask the corpsmen and the medics—those responsible for looking after casualties—to do this at all.

They will become carriers of these same diseases as they go from victim to victim treating each one and spreading this disease in turn from one to the other.

A young Marine in front of me one hot day virtually disappeared; was atomized by an artillery blast that blew him into tiny fragments, and as I looked around the thirty-odd Marines around me we were all covered with part of him—his blood, his flesh, his bones. He was completely on all of us. Had he been AIDS infected, we in turn would have all become infected as well. Over thirty Marines would have become casualties and possibly lost our lives because of this gross irresponsibility that you would now impose on us.

I haven't even addressed the extraordinary burden on an already over-burdened health care system in the military that would look after these diseases and homosexuals.

We do not have enough medical care, enough doctors, enough hospitals to treat so-called normal diseases and injuries which occur on a regular basis. Go in any military hospital today and look at the waiting room and the long lines where military men and their families wait hours upon hours just for normal treatment. You, by the way, are responsible for that.

It is your charge to make that better and yet it continues to get worse. Just imagine what would happen when you add the equation of treatment of homosexuals who have, as we know, over two-thirds of all current AIDS cases.

Let me now address the greatly erroneous myth that homosexuals will obviously be accepted once the President decrees that it be so, and we simply apply better leadership. We already know from the TROA Gallup poll I mentioned that well over 80% refuse to accept that this is the right thing to do. They do not want to remove the ban. A September 1992 USA Weekend Survey of non-military respondents, over two-thirds responded that they wanted the ban to continue. There are many, many other such surveys and none of them yet have said that even half of the American public feels this is the right thing to do. So one must ask, "who wants this to happen, and who will support it?" Well normal Americans, decent Americans will simply not support this kind of activity. They will prevent their children, sons and daughters, from joining the military.

Another survey showed that over 75%—knowing that homosexuals are in the military—would not advise or permit their children to join. No Pentagon policy or any

Congressional mandate, certainly no Presidential decree can change the American public's mind. You may change law and you may change policy but you cannot change the overwhelming, the extraordinary percentage of Americans who feel that this activity is simply unacceptable, and I'll use a term one never hears anymore, indecent. Americans are decent, God-fearing people. They do not consider homosexuality to be decent, normal or acceptable, and they will not permit their children to be around those who have a propensity or even exposure to this type of conduct; therefore, your military will become one of deviants, deviant from the American norm. It may be called an alternate life style; we call it a perversion of normality. It is a perversion of nature, it is a perversion of God's law, it is a perversion of statutory law.

Any attempt to change that will never sit still with the American people. Certainly not for one to two percent of the population. This will not hold. Decent Americans are telling you this and I beg that you listen. Don't change the military which has served you so well—you and the American people—made in the image that you made us, and which has fought and won our nation's wars for over two hundred years. By making this change you will not change us—you will de facto destroy us. I can tell you as a Marine you will virtually destroy the Marine Corps by imposing on us this deviation of values which we hold dear, which we have fought for and which we know to be proper. You are attacking our personal integrity, you are attacking our honor and no military organization can exist without honor and personal integrity. You are asking us to look the other way ignoring a practice we feel deviant, destructive and in conflict with American and God-fearing values. We cannot do this.

I implore you as an American and as a Marine who has fought for his country and loves his Corps and country more than life itself not to lead us into this ambush from which we can never recover.

Colonel Ripley considered the following piece, by TFP author Jeremias Wells, to be the most accurate article of any he had seen describing his actions at the Dong Ha Bridge. The author personally saw numerous copies of this piece in Colonel Ripley's private file cabinet.—Author

Appendix III
"JESUS, MARY, GET ME THERE!"

by Jeremias Wells

INTRODUCTION

When a society no longer respects and honors the fighting men willing to shed their blood for its principles, the fault lies not with the fighting men but with society itself. Ingratitude is a subtle vice, but a vice nevertheless. Saint Thomas Aquinas says that a debt of gratitude is a moral debt required by virtue. In recent decades, the American view of moral justice has been sadly lacking.

Civil society has not always been so callous. Ever since the rise of Christian culture, Christendom has held its warrior-knights in high esteem. Not only that, they were a basic, creative force that molded Western civilization, as a study of the Crusades will attest. A knight of the Middle Ages went to war in a spirit of self-immolation for the glorification of the Church or the common good of temporal society.

Through the centuries, the admiration and appreciation for the fighting man survived a series of revolutionary and philosophical setbacks that severely affected Christendom; that is, until the arrival of communism. As the latter evil gained in influence, a commensurate decline in the will to fight followed. Time and again, the communists won victories because sufficient support from the printed page and the movie and television screens had effectively disarmed the American and Western fighting spirit. Yet the Pattons and MacArthurs of the world continue to step forward, ready to face death rather than betray the ancient ideals of the warrior. The following story represents our part in honoring that crusading spirit.

BACKGROUND

At the end of World War II, the United States and its allies began a series of appeasements to communism that virtually insured more armed conflict. In China a civil war broke out between the communists and the government of China under Generalissimo Chiang Kai-shek, who had been our staunch ally against the Japanese. Under the guise of unity, the United States insisted that the communists be brought into the government. When Chiang refused, George C. Marshall, initially ambassador to China, then Secretary of State, cut off all aid to him despite the fact that the communists were being amply supplied by the Russians. As a result, the communists took over all of China.

This proved to be disastrous for future Pacific engagements, for the Reds now had a large reservoir of trained, well-armed men to draw upon. As a result of World War II treaties, Korea was divided between the communist North and the American-supported South. In 1950 the North Korean Army stormed over the border and was on the verge of throwing all Free World troops into the sea when General Douglas MacArthur personally took charge. In a brilliant and carefully concealed maneuver, he made a surprise amphibious landing at the port of Inchon under extremely difficult circumstances and eventually drove the North Koreans all the way to China. When the Chinese communists moved into position to counterattack, MacArthur was flatly told not to make any bombing runs against their staging areas or in any way hinder their lines of supply and communication. President Truman subsequently fired the "Old Soldier" for publicly declaring that in warfare there is no substitute for victory. His replacement was succeeded by General Mark Clark, who signed an armistice in 1953 with the original borders restored. General Clark lamented that he was the first United States Army commander in history to sign an armistice without victory.

During the early 1960s, the communists moved against South Vietnam, which was also divided between the communist North and the anticommunist South. The scenario was roughly the same. By March 1969, the United States had a troop strength in South Vietnam of 541,500. At no time did the American forces make any determined effort to destroy the enemy's capacity for making war. When Richard Nixon entered the White House in January of 1969, he was principally concerned with withdrawing American troops and getting North Vietnam to the peace table. North Vietnam was principally concerned with crushing its enemy.

In studying the peace negotiations of this period, one could easily be lulled into accepting the sophism that to save lives was worth a compromise with the communists. That may seem reasonable only when we forget the famous and oft-quoted warning of Pius XI: "We cannot contemplate without sorrow the heedlessness of those who seem to make light of these imminent dangers, and with solid indifference allow the propagation far and wide of those doctrines that seek by violence and bloodshed the destruction of all society." The enemies of Christendom never stop; they continue to forge ahead peacefully or otherwise. During the Easter Offensive in 1972, Colonel (at the time Captain) John Ripley and the 3rd Vietnamese Marine Battalion decided to step into the process and bar the way.

THE ATTACK

By the Spring of 1972, the North Vietnamese Army (NVA) had completed its buildup and was ready to mount a largescale attack on South Vietnam. As part of the assault, two infantry divisions, 30,000 soldiers with tanks and artillery support, began to cross the boundary between the two countries and attack south along Highway 1, the main north-south artery. They would first have to seize a highway bridge over the major water obstacle, the Cua Viet River just north of the town Dong Ha. Only the 3rd South Vietnamese Marine Battalion was in a position to block the critical avenue of attack and buy some valuable time. To the 700-man battalion was entrusted the awesome task of stopping, or at least hindering, 30,000 North Vietnamese.

The small number of remaining Americans now in ground combat were assigned to South Vietnamese units as advisers. Few men were better qualified to provide assistance in this nearly impossible assignment than Captain John Ripley of Radford, Virginia. A graduate of the Naval Academy at Annapolis, he led a rifle company through a year of intense combat in 1967. Ripley then served an exchange tour with the British Royal Marines. After returning to U.S. forces, he graduated from both the Army's Airborne and Ranger schools and trained with the Navy's frog men in underwater demolition teams.

Having trained in four elite units, Ripley now joined one of the finest units in the Vietnamese Marine Corps, itself an elite division. Major Le Ba Binh commanded the 3rd Battalion and had a record every bit as impressive as his American adviser. Wounded on a dozen occasions and decorated many times, he was noted for leading his men from the front as would be expected from a member of the aristocratic warrior class.

The 3rd Battalion was composed of four rifle companies.

Two of them and Captain Ripley spent the night before Easter Sunday at an abandoned combat base just west of Dong Ha. The NVA knew they were there, for they pounded the compound all night long with heavy artillery fire. The rounds came screaming in four or five a minute. The Vietnamese got little sleep; Ripley none.

As the day dawned with an overcast sky, Ripley went out and examined the shell craters. The artillery fire was being directed away from the camp toward Dong Ha. He called his radio man to give a report to his own headquarters. Nha, the young baby-faced Vietnamese, approached with long-range whip antenna waving back and forth. In the months they had fought together, the two had become inseparable. Neither knew the other's language well, but facial expressions and a common danger made words unnecessary. By that time Nha could read Ripley's mind.

Ripley grabbed the handset. Headquarters relayed the orders, "Fall back on Dong Ha and defend the bridge. I'll give you more information when I can." Binh's bodyguard, a powerfully built, rough individual who was known as "Three-fingered Jack," appeared and told Ripley that Binh wanted him at his command post. Jack was one of those quiet and alert veterans that command respect; a fearful enemy and a welcome ally.

Binh had decided to deploy the two immediately available companies along the south bank of the Cua Viet River. One company would cover the main bridge used by the north-south traffic along Highway 1. It had been built by the Sea Bees five years earlier to carry the heaviest American weapons and equipment, including tanks. The other company would cover a much older bridge just upstream that could only carry light equipment. Binh told his Marines to dig their holes deep. There would be no fall back positions. They had to hold the riverbank.

The two companies formed a column with Binh and Ripley

leading the way and headed for the bridge. Another radio message warned, "No time for questions, expect enemy tanks. Out." When they reached Highway 9, which ran along the south riverbank and intersected with Highway 1 at Dong Ha, it was clogged with thousands of refugees and, what was worse, deserters by the hundreds. All of them had only one thought in mind: to get as far away as quickly as possible.

Binh's radio contact informed him that the rest of his battalion plus a regular Army of The Republic of Vietnam (ARVN) tank battalion of about 40 tanks would rendezvous with them one mile west of the town. The medium tanks would be somewhat outgunned by the heavier Soviet T-54s, but they were certainly better than no tank support at all. The tank battalion commander, an ARVN lieutenant colonel, was waiting at the rendezvous point with his American adviser, Major James Smock. The former was less than enthusiastic about staying around and required constant urging to cooperate.

Nha approached Ripley. It was headquarters again: "Our outposts can hear the tanks coming. They are traveling in the scrub terrain just off the roadway, but sooner or later they are going to have to get back on Highway 1 to cross the bridge."

"Don't we have any air up, to tell how many?" Ripley asked.

"None yet. Low ceiling."

"Come on. We must have a thousand feet here."

"Believe me, pal, we are doing all we can. Every fire base up there is catching it and some have gone under. You have to hold the bridge and you have to do it alone. There is nothing here to back you up with."

Ripley's American adviser contact continued to give him bad news. Practically all resistance north of the bridge had been wiped out, which was probably the source of the ARVN deserters clogging the road along with the refugees. Then came the final blow: "We finally got a spotter plane in the air. They have tanks and armored personnel carriers stretched along Highway 1 for miles. Must be at least two hundred."

Ripley shouted back, "We can't stop that many. We have to blow the bridge at Dong Ha." At first his superior on the radio hesitated. The top brass back in Saigon wanted to save the bridge. In the end, Ripley's logic prevailed. A weary voice responded: "You are right. We can't authorize it, but you have to blow that bridge. Get moving that way and we will send some demo up to you."

As they approached Dong Ha, they saw the results of the destructive firepower of the enemy's heavy artillery. Corpses lay dismembered and forgotten along the roadside. Dead live-stock and overturned carts were strewn in all directions. Then the artillery started again, countless guns firing together and shells exploding all over the town but only the town. It was being blasted off the map. Everything came to a halt along the highway.

The tank column could not go forward and it could not stay where it was. They backed off to the west and swung around to the southeast and entered what was left of the town from the south. The shelling alternately intensified and then thinned out. At the outskirts, the tank commander refused to go any further but after more arguments agreed to let two tanks accompany the dynamiters. As a parting remark, Binh told Ripley to send a message to his superiors: "There are Vietnamese Marines in Dong Ha. We will fight in Dong Ha. We will die in Dong Ha. As long as one Marine draws a breath of life, Dong Ha will belong to us." A hundred yards from the south end of the bridge, Ripley, Smock and Nha prepared to go on alone.

THE BRIDGE

Captain Ripley studied the bridge through his binoculars. It was built simply but massively. The bridge's basic strength lay in its steel I-beam girders that held up the superstructure. They ran longitudinally, that is, in the direction that the traffic would flow. Each girder stood three feet high, and the flanges extended three to four inches on either side of the vertical member. There were six of them across with about three feet between them. With all that steel, Ripley thought to himself, the Sea Bees could have built a battleship.

These hundred-foot long girders sat on top of massive, steel-reinforced concrete piers (intermediate supports) that rose 20 or 30 feet out of the river. At both sides of the river, the hundred-foot spans connected with the abutments (end supports). In thickness, the piers ran between five and six feet. They would easily have withstood any explosive power then available. The trick was to set the explosives in such a way as to knock one set of girders off the piers, thus dropping a hundred-foot span into the river—no small task but possible by a soldier with the proper training. Fortunately, Captain Ripley had received the necessary training at Ranger School.

Ripley surveyed the scene directly in front of him. Along the near river bank, two companies of Binh's Marines were dug in. Across the river on the north side, there had to be thousands of NVA troops infesting the area. Halfway down his slope, sat a bunker built up with sand bags left over from some previous battle.

The three stood up and made a dash for the bunker. As they ran, the fire from the north side increased in intensity and accuracy. They dove for the bunker just in time. Several shots thudded into the sand bags right in front of them. Ripley decided to leave Nha here, where he could make reports to headquarters just as easily, and not expose him to any more danger than necessary.

He then attracted the attention of a squad leader at the river bank. Through sign language, he asked him to provide cover for the last leg of the journey to the bridge abutment. In a short period of time, Binh's Marines had a steady base of fire hitting NVA positions on the north bank.

The two officers broke from cover and ran straight for the bridge. Again the fire increased as they neared their objective. A heavy tank machine gun kicked a spray of dirt in front of them. Ripley drove himself harder and harder. When he safely reached the bridge abutment, he almost collapsed from the exertion. He wondered how much longer he would have to keep going.

THE DEMOLITION

The explosives were waiting for them, about a dozen pine boxes and an equal number of canvas haversacks. Ripley read the stencil on the three-foot boxes: DEMOLITION-TNT. Each box contained 150 blocks that looked like gray industrial soap. The haversacks contained plastic explosives to be used in conjunction with the TNT.

Ripley decided to cut the girders loose at the first pier, a hundred feet from the abutment. His problems began immediately. The Sea Bees, to prevent sabotage to the under section of the bridge, had constructed a chain-link fence on the river side of the abutment topped with three coils of razor wire. Ripley had to crawl over the razor wire.

He chose to work on the downstream side of the bridge. Most of the infantrymen on both banks had dug in upstream, where they had more open space. The Marine captain climbed the fence and grabbed the bottom flanges of the I-beam. He then swung his feet up and hooked his feet on the flange.

He began to inch himself along the beam. His legs took a beating. The razor wire sliced numerous cuts into his legs which bled profusely. Through the wire he went. He was sweating heavily. The sweat rolled into his cuts and they began to burn. At last, he was through the wire.

With 90 feet to go, Ripley let his feet drop free and proceeded by hand-walking down the girder, swinging forward hand to hand. Arriving at the pier, he made an attempt to catapult himself up into the space between the outboard girder and the next one upstream. His legs would not cooperate. His energy was gone. Hanging only from his hands, they began to ache. Either he flipped up between the two beams soon or he would fall into the river. Once again; he almost made it that time. On the third try the heels caught the flanges. Then he twisted around until his body was spread-eagled between the two beams. He set the two haversacks of satchel charges and crawled on his elbows and knees back to Major Smock and the fence.

The major passed the first two boxes of TNT and two more haversacks through the razor wire, which cut the major's hands and arms. Spread-eagled between the two girders, Ripley placed the boxes on the flanges and dragged the load, which weighed more than 180 pounds, back to the pier, where he set the charges to the first boxes of explosives.

Once more he dropped down, holding onto the bottom flanges with only his hands. Swing back and forth, build momentum, leap, grab, catch the heels and then muscle into the channel opening between the next two girders. When his legs and lower body fell below the beams, the communist riflemen fired up into the steel girders, with rounds ricocheting all over. Nothing hit him. Once up into the channel he was safe.

For the next two hours, Ripley worked his way back and forth setting the charges. When he finished, he crawled back through the razor wire, dropped to the ground and lay there for a while gasping for breath. Yet he had only accomplished the first part of the heroic undertaking. The exhausted Marine had to go out there again and set the detonators.

Ripley would have preferred to use electrical blasting caps and wire, but none were to be found, only the old-fashioned percussion caps and primer cord. To make things more difficult, they could not find any crimpers. Ripley had to crimp the caps onto the cord with his teeth. Since the shiny cylinders would explode if gripped too hard in the wrong place, a slight miscalculation would blow his skull apart. He remembered that back in Ranger School an instructor had placed a detonator inside a softball and set it off. The explosion blew the cover, stuffing and string all over the place.

Carefully he placed the cap into his mouth, open end out and put the primer cord in the open end. He slowly bit down. It worked. The second time would be easier, but he had to fight off overconfidence, so he remembered the softball. Now the Marine captain was ready to go back out again.

This time the enemy was waiting for him. He crawled through the razor wire and dropped below the girder. The communists immediately opened fire, far heavier than before with hundreds of rounds bouncing off the girders. Over and over, he prayed to Our Lord Jesus Christ and His Blessed Mother, "Jesus and Mary, get me there! Jesus and Mary, get me there..."

Just as he reached the upstream box of TNT, a tank shell hit the girder about two feet away. The angle was too flat and it bounced off and exploded on the south bank with a violent crash. The vibrations almost knocked him into the river. He set the detonator into the plastic explosive and lit the other end of the cord with a match. He had measured enough cord to allow about thirty minutes.

The girders of the Dong Ha bridge were three feet high and about three feet apart.

Ripley worked his way over to the downstream side and repeated the process and then hand-walked back to the fence.

He realized that he had exceeded all normal human endurance, so again turned to God and His Mother: "Jesus and Mary, get me there! Jesus and Mary, get me there..." He climbed back through the razor wire once more and fell to the ground near the abutment in a bloody heap. He was so tired that he could hardly lift his arm.

The major tapped him on the back. "Look what I found. But you won't need them now." He pointed to a box of electrical detonators. Ripley looked at the caps and realized that he had to go through the ordeal under the bridge once again. He had always been taught to rig up a backup charge if one was available. At this point, the substance of a man takes over. His moral integrity triumphs. In fact, throughout the entire ordeal, it was the guiding principle. So he returned again simply because to do the job right demanded it.

While Ripley was again risking his life crawling around underneath the Dong Ha Bridge setting up the backup charges, Smock ran a couple of boxes of TNT down to the smaller bridge and ran back again. Ripley had completed the wiring and lay on the ground next to the abutment, too tired to move. Painfully, he pulled himself up and, with a roll of detonating wire hung over his shoulder, staggered along with Smock back to the bunker where Nha was waiting. The South Vietnamese Marines unleashed a barrage of fire to cover them, yelling encouragement as they went, "Dau-uy Dien! Dau- uy Dien!" (Captain Crazy! Captain Crazy!).

At the bunker Ripley was glad to be reunited with Nha. He looked around for a way to trigger the explosion since they had no blasting box. Nearby was a burned-out truck, but the battery appeared to be in good condition. Ripley tried several combinations to set off the explosives. Nothing worked. The terrible thought of failure came over him.

The captain would have to warn headquarters to give time

to others to regroup farther south. He would stay with the 3rd Marine Battalion. Binh would never pull back. He had already made that clear. The battle-scarred warrior would die at his post with no forethought of death. From across the river, Ripley heard the tanks starting up. The massive assault was ready to begin.

Then the bridge blew. The shock waves came before the noise. The noise arrived, growing louder and louder in a series of explosions that became one huge roar. The entire hundred-foot span dropped into the river, leaving a huge gap in the bridge. The time fuses had done their job after all.

THE AFTERMATH

The battle continued to rage around Dong Ha for days after, but the overwhelming forces of the NVA soon began to wear out the defenders. Most areas in the north and south had crumbled. A large group of communists were pressing down on Dong Ha from the west. Binh's Marines were still dug in and holding, with some of Smock's tanks and armored personnel carriers lending support. Ripley was making desperate calls for artillery support when a barrage of mortar fire raked the area, signaling an all-out attack.

At that moment, a vehicle carrying seven journalists and cameramen raced up. Completely oblivious to what was going on, they jumped out and surrounded Captain Ripley with microphones, asking one silly question after another. Ripley yelled at them, "Get out of here; the NVA are attacking." A mortar round exploded, throwing all of them into a pile on the ground. Ripley crawled out from underneath the bodies. Some were dead; others lay groaning and bleeding.

He looked around; then his heart fell. Nha lay dead with a mortar fragment in his head. Major Smock was severely wounded. All the South Vietnamese vehicles were pulling out.

Ripley was able to pile the wounded on them only with difficulty. Nobody was staying around now.

When he went to load Nha's body on the last tank, it moved away and disappeared. The beleaguered captain looked up and saw the point men of several NVA rifle squads approaching. He was going to die, but he was taking his dead radio man with him. He put Nha's body over his shoulders and started walking, fully expecting to catch a bullet any minute.

He heard rifle fire and looked up. Three-fingered Jack and another Marine were firing away at his assailants. More South Vietnamese Marines came over the embankment directly in front of him and kept the enemy pinned down until he climbed up behind them. Captain Ripley was safe.

A few days later the 3rd Marine Battalion received orders to break through the encircling enemy and a few weeks after that it was pulled out of action. Of the original 700 men, only 52 survived. By then Nha and Jack were dead. However, they had succeeded magnificently in their task.

The ARVN regrouped and held a defensive line ten miles south of Dong Ha. Thus the Easter Offensive was stopped because the NVA failed to cross the bridge at Dong Ha. One cannot but wonder that, if a few more men like Captain Ripley, Major Binh, Major Smock, Three-fingered Jack and Nha, the radio man, had dedicated themselves like the Crusaders of old, the communists could have been stopped entirely. As it was, they were stopped for three years.

ABOUT THE AUTHOR

Norman Fulkerson was raised in Red Hill, Kentucky and is a 25-year veteran of the American Society for the Defense of Tradition, Family and Property (TFP). He is a contributing editor to the TFP's *Crusade Magazine* with a current circulation of 130,000. In his "Only in America" column, he describes the little-known cultural richness of the United States. He has also written for the illustrious fifty-year-old Brazilian periodical *Catolicismo*.

He now resides at the TFP headquarters in Spring Grove, Pennsylvania.

BIBLIOGRAPHY

- Colonel Gerald Turley, *The Easter Offensive: The Last American Advisors, Vietnam 1972* (Annapolis, Md.: US Naval Institute Press, 1995).

- John Grider Miller, *The Bridge at Dong Ha* (Annapolis, Md.: United States Naval Institute Press, 1989).

- Plinio Corrêa de Oliveira, *Nobility and Analogous Traditional Elites in the Allocutions of Pius XII* (Lanham, MD.: Hamilton Press, 1993).

- Major Ted McKeldin, USMCR, *From the Horse's Mouth: Selected Thoughts on Small Unit Leadership* (Quantico, Va.: Marine Corps Association, 1999).

- Otto Lehrack, *No Shining Armor: The Marines at War in Vietnam: An Oral History* (Lawrence, Ks.: University Press of Kansas, 1992).

- Richard Botkin, *Ride the Thunder: A Vietnam War Story of Honor and Triumph* (Santa Monica, Ca.: WND Books, 2009).

- Donald Price, *First Marine Captured in Vietnam* (Jefferson, N.C.: McFarland, 2007).

- TFP Committee on American Issues, *Defending a Higher Law: Why We Must Resist Same-Sex "Marriage" and the Homosexual Movement* (Spring Grove, Penn.: The American Society for the Defense of Tradition, Family and Property, 2004).